CANADA

THE
NEXT ONES
HOCKEY'S FUTURE STARS

CANADA

CHL
Canadian Hockey League

THE
NEXT ONES
HOCKEY'S FUTURE STARS

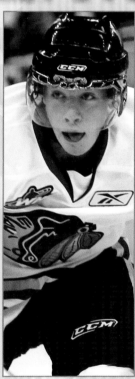

LORNA SCHULTZ NICHOLSON

FOREWORD BY **PAT QUINN**   INTRODUCTION BY **BOB NICHOLSON**

FENN
Fenn Publishing Company Ltd.
Toronto, Canada

Fenn Publishing Company Ltd.

The Next Ones: Hockey's Future Stars

A Fenn Publishing Book / First Published in 2010
All rights reserved
Copyright © Lorna Schultz Nicholson

The content, opinion and subject matter contained herein is the written expression of the author and does not reflect the opinion or ideology of the publisher, or that of the publisher's representatives.

Fenn Publishing Company Ltd.
Toronto, Ontario, Canada
www.hbfenn.com

The publisher gratefully acknowledges the support of the Canada Council for the Arts and the Ontario Arts Council for its publishing program. We acknowledge the support of the Government of Ontario through the Ontario Media Development Corporation's Ontario Book Initiative.

 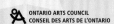

THE CANADA COUNCIL | LE CONSEIL DES ARTS
FOR THE ARTS | DU CANADA
SINCE 1957 | DEPUIS 1957

ONTARIO ARTS COUNCIL
CONSEIL DES ARTS DE L'ONTARIO

We acknowledge the financial support of the Government of Canada through the Canada Book Fund (CBF) for our publishing activities. Care has been taken to trace ownership of copyright material in this book and to secure permissions. The publishers will gladly receive any information that will enable them to rectify errors or omissions.

Cover & Text design: First Image
Printed and bound in Canada

Library and Archives Canada Cataloguing in Publication
Schultz Nicholson, Lorna
   The next ones : hockey's future stars / Lorna Schultz Nicholson.
ISBN 978-1-55168-380-5
   1. Hockey players—Canada—Biography. I. Title.
GV848.5.A1S34 2010   796.962092'2   C2010-902032-4

10 11 12 13 5 4 3 2 1

Contents

CANADA

Foreword

By Pat Quinn

My coaching career has definitely been a lengthy one. I have coached many hockey players over the years but I can honestly say that some of my most enjoyable games on the bench have been with the young Hockey Canada kids. I call them kids because that's what they were when I coached them. I was fortunate enough to coach a Canadian Under-18 team to a gold medal in 2008 in Kazan, Russia and a World Junior team to a gold medal in 2009 in Ottawa, Ontario. Because I coached the Under-18 team first, I had the good fortune of working with many of the same players on both teams.

My first impression with the Under-18 players was that I didn't expect them to be so mature. I expected them to be kids. Their enthusiasm and excitement to represent their county went well beyond my expectations and that has stuck in my mind. It still does when I think back to those championships. Their intent to share what I had to offer was at a level higher than most pro players. It was pleasant coaching amateurs who wanted to be there and be sponges. They were a captive audience and they wanted to listen and learn to become better players.

The challenges I faced coaching these two teams was different. For the players in Ottawa, I knew that they were playing at home in front of a Canadian crowd and that can be intimidating for any hockey player. I had to ask myself, How do I help them learn control? How do kids learn to handle their excitement and the crowd wanting them to win? We talked about focus and playing their game and not letting the crowd dictate how they play. We also talked about how to deal with winning. Each day we spent time talking about these issues. For the younger group we were overseas and travelling long distances does come with its own complications. Plus, some of these kids had never played for Canada. In our country, wearing the Canadian jersey comes with big boots to fill.

The Next Ones, is about young players. Each player in this book has been highlighted because he has been that eager-to-learn sponge. All I can say is this… boys, keep being sponges because it will keep you excited about the great game of hockey and it will make you a better pro player and Hockey Canada player. You've still got a lot to learn and a long way to go and your journey has just started. Believe me when I say it will be filled with excitement and disappointments. That's hockey. And don't I know that. But if you keep learning you will keep improving. And if you keep improving you'll increase your chances to play pro hockey. I look forward to seeing where you boys will end up down the road. Good luck to each and every one of you.

Introduction

By Bob Nicholson

Hockey Canada is so proud of the number of great players we have developed in all positions within our structure of the game. Our player pool has never been better or deeper than at the present time. This is a result of the many volunteers in minor hockey who spend countless hours with the players. We have much-improved coaching in minor hockey and at the junior level and this has had a significant impact on the young players of today. The players of today have taken their hockey to a new level by making an extra special commitment to bettering themselves by working hard on their individual skills on the ice as well as increasing their strength, fitness, and agility off the ice. The players in this book have demonstrated that they are willing to go the extra mile to accomplish their goals in the game of hockey. These players have been supported by their parents who also deserve a lot of credit as these parents have made huge sacrifices allowing their children to play our sport. Canada is filled with many, many parents who support their young hockey players.

Most of the players in this book have been through Hockey Canada's Program of Excellence. The Program of Excellence is now recognized as one of the best programs in the world in any sport. This program continues to improve because of Canada's greatest resource in the game of hockey, and that is its people; the people who continue to come back year after year and graciously give their time to make our country a leader in this game. Hockey Canada is proud of everyone who has made the Program of Excellence better starting with the Under-17, Under-18, and National Junior Team, and recognizes the Canadian Hockey League as a great partner.

I wish all the players in this book, and all the players out there who are working hard, the best of luck in the future and I honestly feel we could have put many books like this together with the amount of talented young players we have in our system.

Go hard boys! Hockey Canada wants quality players like you to play on its teams.

CANADA

Preface

By Lorna Schultz Nicholson

The hardest part about writing *The Next Ones* was creating the list, choosing the young hockey players to be featured in this book. Canada has many amazingly talented young hockey players and I couldn't possibly put them all in one book, unless I wanted to write a book the size of *War and Peace*. And let's face it, in our world today, it's hard to find the time to sit down and read a book this size.

So…this book was written in the Now. And my Now was the spring of 2010. I compiled my information in the spring and the book went to print at the end of the summer. I do realize that even over one summer, a few months, young hockey players do change; they grow, they put on weight, they train, so it is possible that come fall I missed "that" player. I totally understand that at this age, changes occur each and every day. A player who is on top in the fall may not be in the spring and a player who is on top in the spring may not train hard enough or grow enough in the summer to stay on top the next fall. Or a player who is not on top all through the year can suddenly grow and train and emerge out of nowhere. Injuries are also a factor and if a player happened to be injured when I was making my list then they also may not have been given a fair shot. I consulted with many "hockey people" to come up with this list and I went through many, many lists before I came up with this final one.

What I have tried to compile is a list of young Canadian players who have the right combination of skills to play for Hockey Canada and to have a long pro career. Most in the book have already begun their

CANADA

Hockey Canada careers by being part of either an Under-17 or an Under-18 team or both. That said, I have included a few players who haven't yet donned the red and white jersey because there are always those "late bloomers" in hockey. Those players may make a World Junior team when they are nineteen or even when they are about to turn twenty.

And it is very possible that I have left someone out of this book who, at this time in their career, only has pro potential. That is not to say they will never play for a Hockey Canada team as there is no formula for success in hockey, except continual hard work.

In the book, I have mostly included 2010 Draft picks but I also added in some players who will be eligible for the 2011 NHL Entry Draft. Please, keep this book as a guide to refer back to in June of 2011 to see if any of the players chosen for the book are still on top of their game.

I feel extremely lucky that I was able to write a book about such talented young men and I had such terrific help from each and every parent. I truly hope that all the players featured in this book will go on to see continued success in their lives and in their hockey as the commonality in all of them was their work ethic, focus, and passion for the game.

I hope you enjoy learning about these young men as much as I enjoyed writing about them. I certainly enjoyed researching their stories and talking to their parents and coaches to find out how amazing they really are. So relax and enjoy reading about some great kids who are aspiring to be Canada's "Next Ones."

Louis Domingue

CANADA

Catches: **Right**

Height: **6'3"**

Weight: **183 lbs**

Birthdate: **March 6, 1992**

Birthplace: **St-Hyacinthe, Quebec**

Hometown: **Mont St-Hilaire, Quebec**

Team: **Quebec Remparts, QMJHL**

MHA: **Richelieu, Quebec**

2010 NHL Entry Draft:
5th Round, 138th Overall, Phoenix Coyotes

This tall, athletic, right-hand catching goalie has definitely seen some success in his young career. Louis Domingue has won a gold medal playing for Hockey Canada and has been a contributing player in the QMJHL. He went in the 5th round, 138th overall in the 2010 NHL Entry Draft to the Phoenix Coyotes. Although his name didn't appear in the spring of 2010 on the National Junior Team summer camp selection roster, this young netminder is not off the radar. He is still in the mix and much will depend on his play in the fall of 2010.

Louis didn't start playing hockey at the age of five like most other Canadian kids. The Domingue family kept their weekends free to travel so they never pushed Louis into any competitive sports, particularly hockey. That said, he did participate in various sports, such as swimming and baseball, that did not require extensive time commitments.

So when eight-year-old Louis announced at a family dinner in late April that he wanted to play hockey, his parents were confused—the season was over and many of his friends who played hockey had already been playing for two years.

But they agreed to let him give hockey a try. To prepare for his debut in the fall, Louis spent hours outside practising street roller hockey by himself because all his friends had finished their hockey season and had moved on to spring sports. He spent so much time on his in-line skates that he wore the wheels down until sparks lit the air. When his dad took them in to get

Louis started playing hockey at the age of 8 with the Richelieu Minor Hockey Association.

Celebrating winning gold at the Memorial of Ivan Hlinka in 2009.

Q & A

repaired, the store owner laughed and asked if he could keep them because he'd never seen wheels that were so worn before.

That fall, Louis started off as a defenceman and moved to goalie partway through the year when his team was losing and the coach asked to see if anyone else would like a shot playing in net. Louis volunteered, and the team went on to win three straight. Although the coach put him back on defence after those three games, and played him there for the rest of the season, Louis had made his decision. He wanted to be a goalie.

The next season Louis was a full-fledged goalie. He played in net for his team but he also practised on the street, played outdoors on natural ice, attended goalie camps, and solicited help from his grandmother who would shoot foam balls at him from her rocking chair.

Although Louis showed talent and dedication right from the beginning, he did face his share of disappointments. In his first year of peewee he wasn't picked for the AA team and he was confused as to why. He thought he had played well enough to be on the team. His mother then told him, "show them how good you are this year and they will notice you." That was good advice, because in his second year of peewee he made the AA team.

Louis faced big disappointment when he was fifteen. He wanted to play Midget AAA and trained with some of the best players the entire summer before tryouts. In the fall, he was the last one cut from the college midget AAA team where he had been attending Sports-Études for three years. But then the phone call came and he was drafted by West Island in Montreal to play on the Lac Saint-Louis Lions. He started off as the backup goalie, but after just a couple of games was promoted to the starting goaltender, winning the midget AAA Telus Challenge in December and beating a twenty-five-year-old record for number of victories by a rookie, winning twenty-two games.

In the QMJHL entry draft, Louis was selected by the Moncton Wildcats in the first round, 13th overall. At Christmas, a twenty-year-old veteran goalie came back to the Wildcats from the American Hockey League. This was horrible news for Louis because it meant he wouldn't be playing much for the rest of the season. If that wasn't enough, a few days after Christmas, Louis's grandfather, whom he was extremely close to, passed away. At the funeral home, Louis' parents saw him put his hand on his grandfather's heart. When they asked what he was doing, he said, "I'm asking him to help me, if he could." A few days later, Louis received a call from the great Patrick Roy, coach of the Quebec Remparts, a favourite team of his grandfather's. Roy had seen Louis practising in Shawnigan and noticed right away that he had size, athleticism, good hands, and good legs.

Louis didn't disappoint Roy, and he was one of four goalies in the CHL chosen to play in the 2010 CHL/NHL Home Hardware

Top Prospects Game, which took place in Windsor, Ontario. Domingue was on Team Orr; they lost 4–2.

His introduction to Hockey Canada came in 2009, when Louis played for Quebec at the 2009 World Under-17 Hockey Challenge in Port Alberni, British Columbia, finishing fifth. From there he went to the Program of Excellence goaltending camp in Calgary. In August of 2009, Louis attended the Men's National Under-18 Team Summer Selection Camp, making the cut as one of the goaltenders to play at the Memorial of Ivan Hlinka Under-18 tournament in the Czech Republic. He won both games he played and his team brought the gold medal back to Canada. When the Quebec Remparts made it to the second round of the QMJHL playoffs, Louis was unable to commit to playing in the IIHF World Under-18 Championship in Belarus. He was, however, one of the fourteen CHL goalies invited to attend the Hockey Canada Program of Excellence goaltending camp that took place in Calgary in June 2010.

Louis is a tall, strong goalie who has the ability to take up a lot of the net because of his size. He has a good butterfly, quick hands, and a great work ethic which is noticeable to his coach because Louis is always asking to watch his own video replays. With his dominant skills and his positive attitude he is ready to take the next step in his hockey career.

SUMMER UPDATE

Although he wasn't selected to attend the Men's National Junior Team Summer Development Camp in August, Domingue is looking to have a great season in the QMJHL.

Domingue with the Quebec Remparts.

Season	Event	Team	GP	Min	GA	GAA	SO	W	L	T	
					REGULAR SEASON						
2009–10	QMJHL	Quebec Remparts	41	2213	99	2.68	3	20	17	0	
2009–10	QMJHL	Moncton Wildcats	22	1196	56	2.81	1	11	7	2	
2008–09	QMJHL	Moncton Wildcats	12	621	26	2.51	0	5	-5	0	
Totals			75	4030	130	2.53	4	36	29	2	
					PLAYOFFS						
2009–10	QMJHL	Quebec Remparts	9	454.50	33	4.35	0	3	5	0	
					HOCKEY CANADA						
Season	Event	Team	GP	Min	GA	GAA	SO	W	L	T	
2009	WU17	Que	5	265	18	4.08	0	2	2	0	5th
2009	SU18	Can	2	120	2	1.00	0	2	0	0	Gold

Calvin Pickard

Catches: **Left**

Height: **6'1"**

Weight: **202 lbs**

Birthdate: **April 15, 1992**

Birthplace: **Moncton, New Brunswick**

Hometown: **Winnipeg, Manitoba**

Team: **Seattle Thunderbirds, WHL**

MHA: **Winnipeg Minor Hockey Association**

2010 NHL Entry Draft:
2nd Round, 49th Overall, Colorado Avalanche

Two goalies in one family—those are the Pickards. Calvin Pickard, the younger of the two brothers, began playing hockey at the age of five in an initiation program where all budding hockey players play out with no goalie in the net. At the age of seven, he did the usual; sometimes Calvin played forward, sometimes defence, and then when it was his turn, he went in the net. While he liked playing out, Calvin had a natural talent for playing in the net, probably because he had spent time playing hockey with his older brother, Chet, watching him enjoy being a goalie.

Three years later, Calvin tried out for an elite team and was faced with making a choice that would later define him. The league's registration form required the player to select a position: goalie, forward, or defenceman. Calvin was proving to be an incredible goalie, and it seemed that few were as good as him. This would likely see the youngest Pickard get a significant amount of ice time. So, Calvin placed an "X" next to goalie and hasn't looked back since.

Calvin played his early minor hockey in Moncton, New Brunswick. When the Pickard family moved to Winnipeg where he played for the Winnipeg Minor Hockey Association with Fort Garry, his talents allowed him to play a year ahead. His AA and AAA teams were with the Winnipeg Monarchs.

In the 2007 WHL bantam draft, Calvin was selected as the Seattle Thunderbirds' second choice, 38th overall. As a sixteen-

Making a save in an All-Star game.

Stepping on to the ice in a Hockey Canada jersey

Calvin Pickard

Q & A

What is your favourite movie?
Dumb and Dumber

What is your favourite
television show?
Family Guy

What is your favourite book?
Hockey Tough

And your favourite magazine?
The Hockey News

What is your pre-game meal?
Pasta and chicken

What is your favourite
family meal?
Chicken stir-fry

What is your favourite subject
in school?
Physical education

What is your favourite band?
Doc Walker

What are your favourite activities
outside of hockey?
Hanging out with friends,
working out, and
playing golf

Who are your hockey heroes?
Martin Brodeur and
Wayne Gretzky

Who is your hero outside
of hockey?
Terry Fox

What is your most memorable
hockey experience?
Winning the Under-18
Tournament

What's something about yourself
that most people don't know?
I have a little pillow that
I can't sleep without

What is your favourite thing
to do on long bus rides?
Sleep

Who is your favourite superhero?
Spiderman

What is your favourite NHL team?
All of the Canadian teams
and Colorado Avalanche

year-old, he played fifty-four games in his first season in the WHL, impressive considering his age and position. At the beginning of his first season, he was on the roster as the backup goalie, but then the starting goalie with the Thunderbirds was injured so Calvin was called on to fill the spot. He played with such confidence, poise, and guts, that by mid-season, he was Seattle's number one goalie. On October 12, 2008, he was named the CHL goalie of the week, and by the end of the 2008–09 season, Calvin led WHL rookie goaltenders in wins. He finished the season fourth among WHL rookie goaltenders in goals against average and placed third among WHL rookie goaltenders in save percentage. After his first year in the WHL, he had definitely made a name for himself. To put this into perspective, by comparison, Calvin's older brother Chet played twenty-eight games in his first year in the WHL (albeit, he was backup to Carey Price) and went on to be drafted as a first-round selection for the Nashville Predators in 2008. He also won a gold medal with Canada's National Junior Team at the 2009 IIHF World Junior Championship.

Calvin was one of four goalies selected to take part in the 2010 CHL/NHL Top Prospects weekend. He played for Team Cherry and gave up just one goal on fourteen shots, helping lead his team to a 4–2 victory. He also received a few honours at the WHL awards luncheon, winning WHL Goaltender of the Year for the Western Conference and being named to the First All-Star Team for the WHL Western Conference.

Pickard is a smart goalie who reads the play well.

Pickard is one of the top WHL goalies.

Calvin Pickard

CANADA

Calvin is a calm, relaxed goalie and plays consistently, even when bombarded by offensive powerhouses. In his 2009–10 season with the Thunderbirds, Calvin played in many games where he was peppered with numerous shots, and proved himself by playing steady, even hockey. Not as big as his brother, Calvin has spent more time working on his positional play to compensate for his size. This focus is a demonstration of his dedication, and but one example of why Calvin is known as a smart goalie who reads the play well.

Hockey Canada has been impressed with this young man. Calvin attended the Program of Excellence goaltending camp in Calgary in June 2009, and then attended the Men's National Under-18 Summer Selection Camp that August, securing a berth to play at the Memorial of Ivan Hlinka tournament in the Czech Republic. Recently, in the spring of 2010, Calvin competed in the IIHF Men's Under-18 World Championship in Belarus, where the Canadian team finished in an unfortunate seventh place. Following the Hockey Canada path, Calvin had also played with Team West at the 2009 World Under-17 Hockey Challenge in Port Alberni, British Columbia, finishing fourth. In June of 2010, for his second year in a row, Pickard attended the Program of Excellence goaltending camp in Calgary. From that camp, he was invited to attend the 2010 Men's National Junior Team Summer Development Camp.

Calvin looks forward to playing another season with Seattle where he is known as a force for the franchise. In the 2010 NHL Entry Draft, Pickard went in the 2nd round, 49th overall to the Phoenix Coyotes and will attend their rookie camp. The limelight doesn't frighten this young man, he enjoys it. As for his future, watch out for this calm, unflappable young goalie to be a pro one day and indeed grace the international stage again.

SUMMER UPDATE

Pickard played on Team White at the Men's National Junior Team Summer Development Camp in August, winning both games.

Pickard has played on numerous Hockey Canada teams.

The Next Ones

Pickard is a large part of the Seattle Thunderbirds franchise.

Season	Event	Team	GP	Min	GA	GAA	SO	W	L	T
			REGULAR SEASON							
2009–10	WHL	Seattle Thunderbirds	62	3,688	190	3.09	3	16	46	0
2008–09	WHL	Seattle Thunderbirds	47	2,694	137	3.05	3	23	21	0
Totals			109	6382	327	3.07	6	39	67	0
			PLAYOFFS							
2008-09	WHL	Seattle Thunderbirds	5	262	15	3.03	0	1	4	–

			HOCKEY CANADA							
Season	Event	Team	GP	Min	GA	GAA	SO	W	L	T
2010	WU18	Can	6	314	15	2.87	0	5	3	0
2009	SU18	Can	2	120	5	2.50	0	2	0	0
2009	WU17HC	West	5	280	17	3.64	0	3	2	0

Calvin Pickard

Tyson Teichmann

Catches: **Left**

Height: **6'0''**

Weight: **150 lbs**

Birthdate: **May 19, 1993**

Birthplace: **Belleville, Ontario**

Hometown: **Belleville, Ontario**

Team: **Belleville Bulls, OHL**

MHA: **Belleville Minor Hockey**

NHL Draft: **2011 Eligibility**

Every once in a while, a hometown boy playing bantam hockey gets drafted by the hometown junior team. Picking a hometown boy is rare enough, but it was even rarer when the Belleville Bulls picked a goalie. Young goalies are rarely drafted in the 1st round, and the Belleville Bulls took a risk when they selected Tyson Teichmann. But Tyson had wowed the coaches and, as a result, they believed that he was the elite player that they both wanted and needed. They even forced a trade to show that Tyson was their guy.

After one year of junior hockey Tyson continues to impress, especially his coaches. At sixteen, he logged thirty-plus games in his first year in major junior. An ankle injury in the second half of the season slowed Tyson down a bit, though even with the injury, Belleville Bulls head coach, George Burnett, continued to have faith in Tyson's abilities and future. Burnett believes Tyson is amongst the elite, and that he will be their go-to goalie next year— an incredible achievement for a seventeen-year-old. A summer of hard work at the gym will increase his athleticism and put his injury behind him. Tyson's credentials are strong and get stronger every day.

Some goalies end up in the position after giving it a try in their young hockey careers. Tyson, however, knew right from the beginning he wanted to be a goalie. His father had been a goalie, and had even played for the Belleville Bulls. In fact, Tyson was born when his father was still playing in the OHL, so from an

A young Tyson playing with the Belleville Minor Hockey Association.

Focused at the 2010 World Under-17 Hockey Challenge.

Tyson Teichmann

Q & A

early age goaltending was in his blood. Initially, his parents enrolled him in a learn-to-skate program when he was young. Then, after much insisting from young Tyson, his father set up a makeshift net in the garage, complete with carpet for ice and plumber's foam to keep the pucks from creating holes in the wall.

Tyson played two years with Belleville minor hockey then moved to play AAA with Quinte regional minor hockey. His dad coached him for some of his minor hockey career, but that doesn't mean Tyson was pushed to play. He was self motivated and got himself out of bed and ready to head to the rink. Every spring, when the hockey season was over, he played rec soccer to stay in shape. And when the hot days of summer rolled around, instead of lazing and enjoying the heat, he spent much of his time on the ice at the Jon Elkin goalie school to hone his skills. His parents feel that he sacrificed a lot to become the goalie he is today.

At only sixteen, Tyson already stands six feet tall. His weight is slight, at just 150 lbs, though he has a good frame and the full potential to be much bigger in the coming years. He will have to grow physically to see professional success, but his track record to date is impressive and he has created a solid base that could lead to a career as a professional goalie. A competitive drive seems to be innate in Tyson. He hates to lose, even in practice, and this determination will take him a long way.

During the 2010 World Under-17 Hockey Challenge, Tyson proved he had that gritty competitiveness when he played for Team Ontario. At first slotting, he was Team Ontario's backup goalie, but on January 1st he recorded his second straight shutout by turning away twenty-two shots against the previously unbeaten Team Sweden. This shutout earned him the first star of the day. Team Ontario went on to face Team United States in the gold-medal game, but were defeated in a close 2–1 battle. This stellar play helped Tyson earn an invite to Hockey Canada's Program of Excellence goaltending camp in June of 2010. Only fourteen goalies were invited and only five were eligible Under-18 players. At the end of the camp, Teichmann was one of the four goalies in the age group invited to attend the Men's National Under-18 Team Summer Selection Camp in August.

From working with Jon Elkin, Tyson has adopted the butterfly style of goaltending. He knows his angles, and cuts down the shooting lanes well. He challenges the puck carrier, and can grab a shot out of the air with a lightning-fast glove hand.

Every time he gets frustrated, as young players often do, Tyson's coach tells him to keep focused and push through. The Belleville Bulls believe he will be a key player for their team next year, and if he continues on the path he has set, it is likely that Hockey Canada will continue to consider him.

Tyson's draft year is 2011.

Tyson has adopted the butterfly style of goaltending.

CANADA

SUMMER UPDATE
Teichmann was selected as the number one goalie for Hockey Canada's Men's National Under-18 Summer Team and played four games at the Memorial of Ivan Hlinka in the Czech Republic and ended with a 4–0 record, winning gold.

Season	Event	Team	GP	Min	GA	GAA	SO	W	L	T	
REGULAR SEASON											
2009–10	OHL	Belleville Bulls	30	1455	104	4.29	0	6	16	0	
Totals			30	1455	104	4.29	0	6	16	0	

HOCKEY CANADA											
Season	Event	Team	GP	Min	GA	GAA	SO	W	L	T	
2010	WU17HC	Ontario	6	340	9	1.59	2	4	1	0	Silver

Tyson Teichmann

Mark Visentin

CANADA

Catches: **Left**

Height: **6'1"**

Weight: **186 lbs**

Birthdate: **August 7, 1992**

Birthplace: **Hamilton, Ontario**

Hometown: **Waterdown, Ontario**

Team: **Niagara Ice Dogs, OHL**

MHA: **Halton Hills MHA**

2010 NHL Entry Draft:
1st Round, 27th Overall, Phoenix Coyotes

Since January 2010, Mark Visentin has seen a lot of ice time playing in net for the OHL Niagara Ice Dogs, where it seemed that in every practice and every game his skills just kept improving. Mark's climb to the top started two years ago, but in the last half of his 2009–10 season, his play truly developed to an elite level. Mark worked his position hard and for his efforts became the first Canadian goalie drafted in the 2010 NHL Entry Draft. The Phoenix Coyotes picked Mark in the 1st round, 27th overall. This came as a pleasant shock to Visentin and his family. Mark had brought two suits to Los Angeles for the draft weekend—one for each day of the event. On the first day, which is when they announce the first round picks, he told family and friends not to bother coming. He wore his second-round suit. Fortunately, no one listened to him, and when his name was called that first day, they were there to cheer him on.

Mark didn't always love hockey. In fact, halfway through his first year of playing in Waterdown, Ontario, he wanted to quit. But his parents told him that it was important to see through his commitments and that he had to finish off the season. Mark's team rotated goaltending duties and selected each game's netminder through an alphabetical process. With the name Visentin, his time to play didn't come until the end of the season, though that day was a turning point in his career. He came off the ice that day and said, "I love this. I want to do this forever."

Mark's first year of hockey. He only liked the sport when he took a turn in net.

Visentin celebrating at the 2009 World Under-17 Hockey Challenge with Team Ontario.

Q & A

What is your favourite movie?
Happy Gilmore

What is your favourite
television show?
Entourage

What is your favourite book?
Playing with Fire

What is your pre-game meal?
Chicken Parmesan

What is your favourite
family meal?
Alaskan king crab

What are your favourite
subjects in school?
Physical education
and math

What is your favourite band?
Blink 182

What are your favourite activities
outside of hockey?
Tennis, mountain biking,
golf, swimming,
and camping

Who is your hockey hero?
I wouldn't say I have a hero,
but I look up to Cam Ward
and Marc-Andre Fleury

Who is your hero outside
of hockey?
Tiger Woods

What is your most memorable
hockey experience?
Getting drafted by the
Phoenix Coyotes

What's something about yourself
that most people don't know?
I play the drums, and was
in a band before I started
playing junior

What is your favourite thing
to do on long bus rides?
Listen to music on my iPod

What is your favourite NHL team?
Obviously Phoenix!
But I grew up cheering
for the Habs

Mark went on to play in net for the Flamborough Sabres and the Halton Hurricanes. At the OHL 2008 Priority Selection draft, Visentin was disappointed when he was the third goalie selected—he had set his sights on being first. That said, he didn't allow the disappointment to stall his progress, but instead used the experience to push himself to work harder at his game. The Niagara Ice Dogs picked Visentin up in the 3rd round, 54th overall.

During the 2008–09 season—his first year with the Ice Dogs—Visentin started in twenty-three games. It is rare for a sixteen-year-old netminder to see such ice time in the OHL, and while Visentin was pleased with his chances to play, he was not pleased with his team's poor 5–11–2–1 record. Losing record aside, the Ice Dog's coaching staff recognized that they had a talented young goalie on their roster. Mark trained hard that summer and was rewarded with the starting goaltender position that next fall. The Ice Dogs had a young team and struggled the first half of the year, often allowing fifty or more shots on their net. It was an emotional roller coaster for the seventeen-year-old goalie, but Visentin remained focused

Visentin with the Niagara Ice Dogs.

Serious concentration during the singing of *O Canada*.

Mark Visentin

and never lost his determination to win. In the second half of the season, the team picked up their pace and, with a lot of grittiness, they steadily rose from last place to seventh, earning a berth to the playoffs. Mark's record and goals-against average improved, which was good enough to see him chosen to play with Team Orr at the 2010 CHL/NHL Home Hardware Top Prospects Game.

Hockey Canada has also taken an interest in Visentin and it was a year of surprises for the young man. In the spring of 2010, Mark attended Hockey Canada's Program of Excellence goalie camp in Calgary and was one of four goalies invited to attend the Men's National Junior Team Summer Development Camp. In 2008, he played for Team Ontario at the World Under-17 Hockey Challenge in Port Alberni. In 2009, he was invited to attend the Men's National Under-18 Team Summer Selection Camp, though he left disappointed, not making the team that played in the Memorial of Ivan Hlinka.

At 6'1", Visentin is a fairly big player that naturally covers a lot of the net. He has great mobility and side-to-side movement, and because of the many games where he faced fifty-plus shots, he is also a goalie who makes save after save and controls his rebounds well. Known as a workhorse, Mark is constantly trying to improve his game. He is working with a goalie coach on his positioning and learning to better read the play and anticipate the offence's next move. Back with the Niagara Ice Dogs in the fall of 2010, if he continues to stop shot after shot, Mark will undoubtedly have a great future with Hockey Canada and the world of professional hockey.

SUMMER UPDATE

Visentin played on Team Red at the Men's National Junior Team Summer Development Camp in August. Team Red lost both games but Visentin had a strong third period in the second game.

Playing on Team Orr at the CHL/NHL Home Hardware Top Prospects Game.

The Next Ones

Visentin has great mobility and side-to-side movement.

CANADA

Season	Event	Team	GP	Min	GA	GAA	SO	W	L	T	
				REGULAR SEASON							
2009–10	OHL	Niagara Ice Dogs	55	3209	160	2.99	0	24	31	0	
2008–09	OHL	Niagara Ice Dogs	23	1,099	78	4.26	0	5	14	0	
Totals			78	1408	238	3.62	0	29	45	0	
				PLAYOFFS							
2009–10	OHL	Niagara Ice Dogs	5	305	18	3.54	0	1	4	–	
				HOCKEY CANADA							
Season	Event	Team	GP	Min	GA	GAA	SO	W	L	T	
2009	WU17HC	Ontario	1	60	1	1.00	0	1	0	0	Gold

Mark Visentin

Jerome Gauthier-Leduc

CANADA

Shoots: **Right**

Height: **6'1"**

Weight: **181 lbs**

Birthdate: **July 30, 1992**

Birthplace: **Quebec City, QC**

Hometown: **Quebec City, QC**

Team: **Rimouski Océanic, QMJHL**

MHA: **Quebec City MHA**

2010 NHL Entry Draft:
3rd Round, 68th Overall, Buffalo Sabres

Some wonder if players from small, out-of-the-way, Quebec towns get scouted as much as those playing for big-market teams, especially on home ice. Quebec-born defenceman, Jerome Gauthier-Leduc, is known as a good playmaker who can follow the rush and score goals. But there were many scouts unlikely to see any of his home games, as his 2009–10 team, the QMJHL Rouyn-Noranda Huskies' home rink was a ten-hour drive from Quebec City and an eight and a half-hour drive from Montreal. This year being his draft year, it is more than likely that most of his talents were seen at away games, far from his home rink.Still, in the 2010 NHL Entry Draft he went in the 3rd round, 68th overall to the Buffalo Sabres. Gauthier-Leduc was pleased with this result. He was also extremely excited and pleasantly thrilled to have been asked to attend the Men's National Junior Team Summer Development Camp in August of 2010. When the call came he admits that his reaction was pure shock.

But there are good reasons why Jerome was invited to the camp. He is a strong, offensive defenceman and has great agility on his skates. His skilled skating combined with his solid puck-handling makes him a strong contender for Hockey Canada teams.

Jerome played minor hockey with the Quebec Minor Hockey Association, where he racked up many championship wins. In 2007, Gauthier-Leduc was named top defenceman in

A young Jerome before a game.

Playing with Team Quebec at the
2009 World Under-17 Hockey Challenge.

Jerome Gauthier-Leduc

Q & A

What is your favourite movie?
The Hangover

What is your favourite television show?
Two and a Half Men

What is your favourite magazine?
Hockey magazines

What is your pre-game meal?
Pasta

What is your favourite family meal?
Steak and potatoes

What is your favourite subject in school?
Math

Who is your favourite musician?
Eminem

What is your favourite activitiy outside of hockey?
Tennis

Who is your hockey hero?
Kris Letang

Who is your hero outside of hockey?
Raphael Nadal

What is your most memorable hockey experience?
Playing in the Prospect Game in Windsor

What's something about yourself that most people don't know?
I could have been a soccer player

What is your favourite thing to do on long bus rides?
Watching TV shows

Who is your favourite superhero?
Superman

What is your favourite NHL team?
The Buffalo Sabres

his bantam league and also played in the Bantam AA all-star game. The next season, he experienced the thrill of winning the Ligue du hockey midget AAA du Quebec Championship when playing midget hockey on the Séminaire Saint-François Midget AAA team. That same year, (2008), his Midget AAA team also played in the Telus Cup, Canada's National Midget Championship, capturing the bronze medal.

When the 2008 QMJHL draft rolled around, he was chosen by the Drummondville Voltigeurs in the 1st round, 18th overall. Jerome showed up to the Voltigeurs camp in August, and played just one week before he was traded to the Rouyn-Noranda Huskies on September 4th. Camp hadn't even ended and he was packing his bags to head on a ten-hour drive to a copper-mining town in Northern Quebec. Although Gauthier-Leduc understood that Drummondville had their sights set on winning the Memorial Cup, and that he was too young for their team, it was still a huge disappointment to be traded so soon and to a team so far away from home.

Jerome played two years with the Rouyn-Noranda Huskies. In his rookie year, 2008–09, he played in fifty-two games and scored one goal. Adding sixteen assists, he finished the regular season with seventeen points and in six playoff games, he had two more assists.

It was his 2009–10 season that caught scouts' eyes, especially the Hockey Canada scouts, causing them to take a closer look at this young player. In sixty-eight games, Gauthier-Leduc secured twenty goals and twenty-six assists for forty-six points. Those offensive stats were coupled with a +26 rating, making him a player to watch. Then in eleven playoff games, he parked the puck in the net twice and gathered four assists. At the end of the 2009–10 season, Jerome was traded to the Rimouski Océanic—a trade he could definitely live with.

At the 2010 CHL/NHL Home Hardware Top Prospects Game in January, Gauthier-Leduc was invited to play for Team Orr. In the skills competition, he won the hardest-shot contest.

Jerome is no stranger to Hockey Canada teams. In 2008 he played in one exhibition game for Team Quebec at the World Under-17 Hockey Challenge. Then in 2009 he officially made the team and played with Team Quebec, finishing in fifth place. When spring arrived, Hockey Canada invited him to the 2009 Men's National Under-18 Team Summer Selection Camp. Though Gauthier-Leduc didn't make the final roster, he gained a new level of determination from the experience and was set to prove himself the following fall. His hard work paid off, thus the reason why he was on the ice in August at the Men's National Junior Team Summer Development Camp. Look for this young man on future Hockey Canada teams.

CANADA

SUMMER UPDATE
Gauthier-Leduc played on Team White at the Men's National Junior Team Summer Development Camp in August. White won both games.

Gauthier-Leduc in his Rouyn-Noranda Huskies jersey. In the fall of 2010 he will be wearing a Rimouski jersey as he was traded at the end of last season.

Season	Event	Team	GP	G	A	Pts	+/-	PIM	
REGULAR SEASON									
2009–10	QMJHL	Rouyn-Noranda Huskies	68	20	26	46	26	16	
2008–09	QMJHL	Rouyn-Noranda Huskies	52	1	16	17	-20	8	
TOTALS			120	21	42	63	6	24	
PLAYOFFS									
2010	QMJHL	Rouyn-Noranda Huskies	6	0	2	2	0	5	
2009	QMJHL	Rouyn-Noranda Huskies	11	2	4	6	2	2	
TOTALS			17	2	6	8	2	7	
HOCKEY CANADA									
Season	Event	Team	GP	G	A	PTS	+/-	PIM	
2009	WU17HC	Quebec	5	0	2	2	–	0	5th

Brandon Gormley

Shoots: **Left**

Height: **6'2"**

Weight: **184 lbs**

Birthdate: **February 18, 1992**

Birthplace: **Murray River, P.E.I.**

Hometown: **Murray River, P.E.I.**

Team: **Moncton Wildcats, QMJHL**

MHA: **Northumberland MHA**

2010 NHL Entry Draft:
1st Round, 13th Overall, Phoenix Coyotes

When Brandon Gormley was only fourteen years old, he left Murray River, Prince Edward Island, (population two hundred), to pursue his hockey career. His father is a fisherman and Brandon loved going out to sea with his dad. Brandon was heading to a place where there was no ocean for miles—only the fresh water lakes of rural Saskatchewan. That would be a culture shock to anyone, especially a fourteen-year-old, but Gormley had wanted to be a hockey player since he first started skating lessons at the age of three. He understood that he would have to give up a lot for his dream to become a reality. So, he left the fishing, the ocean, his home, and his family to attend Notre Dame in Wilcox, Saskatchewan.

Fortunately, he was billeted with a family originally from PEI, making Brandon's parents happy. Gormley fit right in with the Davies family, and they treated him like a son from day one. Gormley stayed at Notre Dame for two years, playing in the Saskatchewan Midget AAA league until he was eligible for the QMJHL entry draft, at which time Brandon travelled back to the East Coast to attend the draft in Sydney, Nova Scotia. He was drafted 1st overall by the Moncton Wildcats. Brandon was pleased to be returning to the Maritimes and said goodbye to Notre Dame.

Gormley as a youngster playing in P.E.I.

Brandon grew up five minutes from Murray Harbour, home of NHL great, Brad Richards. As a youngster, Brandon often travelled to watch Richards play with Moncton. Richards played a big part in helping Gormley realize that dreams were there to be fulfilled, not forgotten, proving that players from small towns could make it big.

Gormley played in two World Under-17 Hockey Challenges for Team Atlantic.

Brandon Gormley

Q & A

After the QMJHL draft, Brandon took to the ice with the Wildcats and didn't disappoint. He had a great first season, ending up second among the Moncton rookies in scoring, and being named to the QMJHL All-Rookie Team. He was also named the Moncton Wildcats Rookie of the Year and played for Team QMJHL in the ADT Canada-Russia Challenge. Moncton's coach, Danny Flynn, has played Brandon in every game situation, giving the young defencemen extensive ice time. The Moncton Wildcats had a great run in the 2010 race to the Memorial Cup, winning the QMJHL President's Cup trophy and a berth to play in the MasterCard Memorial Cup. Although the Wildcats didn't win the tournament, Brandon ended up tied for most points among the defencemen at the tournament. He definitely helped his team earn the right to play in this prestigious tournament.

For his efforts with the Moncton Wildcats in the 2009–2010 season, at the QMJHL Golden Pucks awards banquet in March of 2010, Gormley won the Trophée Michael Bossy (meilleur espoir), recognizing him as a top professional prospect. Gormley also played for Team Orr at the 2010 CHL/NHL Home Hardware Top Prospects Game in Windsor, Ontario, where he won the fastest skater award for his team in the Home Hardware Skills Competition. He was picked to be an assistant captain for Team Orr, and though his team lost 4–2, in the final game he picked up an assist for the effort.

For such a young player, Gormley's international experience is quite vast as he is just one of a handful of players who has played in two World Under-17 Hockey Challenges. His first foray was for Team Atlantic at the 2008 World Under-17 Hockey Challenge in London, Ontario, where his team finished eighth. He also played in the 2009 World Under-17 Hockey Challenge in Port Alberni, where his team finished ninth overall. After two years of Under-17, he moved into the Under-18 program, making the final team that headed off to the Memorial of Ivan Hlinka tournament in the Czech Republic in August 2009. Brandon would have been a shoo-in for the World Under-18 Championship in the spring of 2010, but the Moncton Wildcats were contenders in the 2010 MasterCard Memorial Cup and he couldn't leave his team.

Recently, he made two extremely big strides in the hockey world. At the 2010 NHL Entry Draft, Gormley was called to the podium by the Phoenix Coyotes as their first-round pick, making him the 13th selection overall. And to top that off, when Hockey Canada sent out their press release naming the forty-one skaters who were invited to their Men's National Junior Team Summer Development Camp in August, Gormley's name was on the list.

Brandon is a hard worker, both on and off the ice. He is known as a two-way player with good feet for a defenceman and poise with the puck. He is a smart player who can move the puck out of trouble quickly.

Playing with Team Canada. Gormley is one of a few players to have played in two Under-17 events.

CANADA

Brandon Gormley

Gormley is a good two-way defenceman.

Gormley with the Moncton Wildcats of the QMJHL.

SUMMER UPDATE
Gormley played on Team Red at the Men's National Junior Team Summer Development Camp in August. Red lost both games.

Season	Event	Team	GP	G	A	Pts	+/-	PIM	
		REGULAR SEASON							
2009–10	QMJHL	Moncton Wildcats	58	9	34	43	31	54	
2008–09	QMJHL	Moncton Wildcats	62	7	20	27	9	3	
TOTALS			120	16	54	70	40	88	
		PLAYOFFS							
2010	QMJHL	Moncton Wildcats	21	2	15	17	14	10	
2009	QMJHL	Moncton Wildcats	10	1	3	4	4	6	
TOTAL			31	3	18	21	18	16	
		HOCKEY CANADA							
Season	Event	Team	GP	G	A	PTS	+/-	PIM	
2009	Memorial of Ivan Hlinka	Under 18	4	3	2	5	–	0	Gold
2009	WU17HC	Atlantic	5	3	3	6	–	2	8th
2008	WU17HC	Atlantic	5	2	1	3	–	4	9th

Erik Gudbranson

CANADA

Shoots: **Right**

Height: **6'4"**

Weight: **198 lbs**

Birthdate: **January 7, 1992**

Birthplace: **Ottawa, Ontario**

Hometown: **Orleans, Ontario**

Team: **Kingston Frontenacs, OHL**

MHA: **Blackburn MHA**

2010 NHL Entry Draft:
1st Round, 3rd Overall, Florida Panthers

Google the name Erik Gudbranson and his long list of hockey achievements will quickly appear—most recently his being selected 3rd overall in the 2010 NHL Entry Draft by the Florida Panthers and his invitation to Canada's 2010 National Junior Team Development Camp.

Along with his Google hits pops up a YouTube video. No, it's not a video highlighting his best fights to date, it's a poignant, heart-wrenching video of a young hockey player talking about his little brother, Dennis, who has recently battled leukemia. He talks about seeing his brother with needles and tubes, and sitting by his hospital bed. Erik talks candidly about the struggles his brother has endured and just how hard it has been for his family to see his brother so sick. He talks of how his brother has fought harder than he will ever have to fight as a hockey player, and concludes the video by sharing that his hero in life is his brother Dennis because he is the toughest fighter he knows.

Erik is the eldest of four children. In addition to Dennis, who is now twelve, Erik has another brother, Alex who is fifteen (he was just picked by the Kingston Frontenacs in the 1st round, 10th overall in the 2010 OHL Priority Selection draft) and a ten-year-old sister, Chantal. When his brother was diagnosed with leukemia, Erik was playing minor hockey, but with his parents spending so much time at the hospital he took on many

Gudbranson is the eldest of four. Here he is when he played minor hockey with Blackburn.

Erik captained Team Ontario
at the 2009 World Under-17
Hockey Challenge.

Erik Gudbranson

Q & A

responsibilities at home in an effort to help out in a time of need. His mother says that, "Erik took on the responsibility in his own quiet way. Erik was born with a briefcase in his hands."

But the fact is, the way this young defenceman plays hockey he must have also been born with a hockey stick in his hands.

According to his coach with the Kingston Frontenacs, Chris Bryne, Erik has all the tools and makings to be a great player. He shoots well, handles the puck well, and has that rare right-handed shot that often tricks goalies. He is also a tremendous skater with a strong, physical presence. With his competitive drive, and that wanting-to-win-at-all-costs attitude, he is the complete package. Like most players his age, he works continuously at polishing his skills by playing as much as he can. He shows up to every game and practice with a rare level of competitiveness and determination.

His parents always encouraged their children to be passionate about extracurricular activities. They taught them that no matter what, they had to give one hundred per cent, and those same expectations were similarly meant for the classroom, where Erik has definitely excelled. Growing up, hockey was a privilege for Erik and not a right so he made sure to maintain good grades, allowing him to play the sport he loved. Coming from a family of four children and with a brother who was hospitalized, Erik kept up his grades by being an autonomous student, working independently.

Erik played minor hockey in Blackburn and Gloucester in the Ottawa area. When he started to play AAA hockey, he moved to the Ottawa Jr. 67's.

The Kingston Frontenacs picked Erik as their first-round selection, 4th overall in the 2008 OHL Priority Selection. In his 2008–09 season he was third among Kingston defencemen in scoring, second among Kingston rookies in scoring, and he led Kingston rookie defencemen in scoring. He was named to the OHL Second All-Rookie team. In his 2009–10 season with the Frontenacs, Gudbranson picked up another twenty-three points in regular season play and claimed the Bobby Smith Trophy as the OHL's Scholastic Player of the Year, with an overall average of eighty per cent.

Hockey Canada took notice of this young defenceman. In 2009, Erik captained Team Ontario to a gold medal at the World Under-17 Hockey Challenge in Port Alberni. Then he played with Canada's National Men's Under-18 Team at the 2009 IIHF World Under-18 Championship in Fargo, North Dakota, where they finished fourth. Only three players from the 1992 birth year were chosen for this team: Erik Gudbranson, Brett Connolly, and John McFarland. In August of 2009, Erik attended the Under-18 camp in Calgary and headed over to the Czech Republic to play in the Memorial of Ivan Hlinka tournament. From that tournament, Erik came home with yet another gold medal. When Kingston was knocked out of the OHL

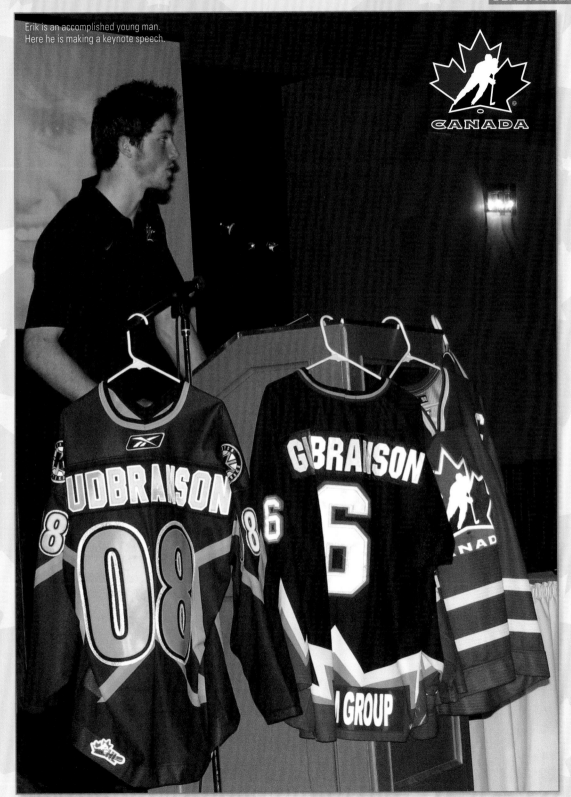

Erik is an accomplished young man. Here he is making a keynote speech.

Erik Gudbranson

CANADA

SUMMER UPDATE

Gudbranson played on Team White at the Men's National Junior Team Summer Development Camp in August. White won both games.

playoff run in the first round by Brampton in seven games, there was still time for Erik to head over to Belarus to play in the 2010 IIHF World Under-18 Championship. Unfortunately that team only managed to muster up a seventh-place finish.

With everything that has happened in his life, and the responsibilities Erik has had to shoulder, he handles himself with maturity no matter where he goes. In the dressing room he possesses a strong level of confidence and is vocal when he needs to be, exhibiting excellent leadership skills.

This young player has been through more than most at his age, and has handled his trials and tribulations with poise, dignity, and a raw honesty. His future is bright, and if he continues to polish his skills and play, his hockey gifts will continue to reward him.

Gudbranson played two years on Canada's Under-18 Team.

Gudbranson is an extremely strong skater for the Kingston Frontenacs.

Season	Event	Team	GP	G	A	Pts	+/-	PIM	
		REGULAR SEASON							
2009–10	OHL	Kingston Frontenacs	41	2	21	23	11	68	
2008–09	OHL	Kingston Frontenacs	63	3	19	22	-16	69	
TOTALS			104	5	40	45	-5	137	
		PLAYOFFS							
2010	OHL	Kingston Frontenacs	7	1	2	3	0	6	
TOTALS			7	1	2	3	0	6	
		HOCKEY CANADA							
Season	Event	Team	GP	G	A	PTS	+/-	PIM	
2010	IIHF World Under-18 Championship	Under 18	4	1	0	1	–	10	7th
2009	Memorial of Ivan Hlinka	Under 18	4	0	1	1	–	2	Gold
2009	IIHF World Under-18 Championship	Under 18	6	1	3	4	–	0	4th
2009	WU17HC	Ontario	6	2	2	4	–	0	Gold

Erik Gudbranson

Alexander Petrovic

CANADA

Shoots: **Right**

Height: **6'4"**

Weight: **193 lbs**

Birthdate: **March 3, 1992**

Birthplace: **Edmonton, Alberta**

Hometown: **Edmonton, Alberta**

Team: **Red Deer Rebels, WHL**

MHA: **Edmonton MHA**

2010 NHL Entry Draft:
2nd Round, 36th Overall, Florida Panthers

A solid two-way defenceman, Alex Petrovic has been a key player for the Red Deer Rebels since he was drafted by them in the 2007 WHL bantam draft. He was a second-round selection, 33rd overall and joined the Rebels in the fall of 2008. Right from the get-go head coach of the Rebels, Jesse Wallin, placed Petrovic in big roles. He faced him against top lines, and top players, where Petrovic held his own—impressive for a sixteen-year-old.

His level of play demonstrated such impressive leadership qualities, that the following year at the age of just seventeen, Petrovic was rewarded with an assistant captain letter, an honour that not many seventeen-year-olds can claim. Although he possesses a serious demeanor in the dressing room, away from the arena he has a great sense of humour and enjoys sharing a laugh with friends and teammates. Maybe it is his positive attitude and ability to laugh and relax that allows him to be so focused on the ice.

At 6'4", Alex is a large boy with a frame that will continue to fill out and provide him with a competitive edge—an edge that the Florida Panthers recognized as they drafted him in the 2nd round, 36th overall in the 2010 NHL Entry Draft. He needs to improve his strength, which he addresses by spending countless hours training in order to get to the next level. When he fills out he is going to have a physicality that few can match, which will make him a serious and imposing threat on the blue line.

A young Alex with one of many trophies he won while playing minor hockey in Edmonton.

Petrovic is a strong blue-liner with the Red Deer Rebels.

Alexander Petrovic

Q&A

What is your favourite movie?
Happy Gilmore

What is your favourite
television channel?
TSN

What is your favourite magazine?
Sports Illustrated

What is your pre-game meal?
Pasta with tomato sauce

What is your favourite
family meal?
**Stuffed green peppers,
made by my dad**

What is your favourite
subject in school?
Sciences

What is your favourite band?
Rush

What are your favourite activities
outside of hockey?
**Hanging out with
friends and family and
playing Xbox**

Who is your hockey hero?
Chris Pronger

Who is your hero outside of
hockey?
Tiger Woods

What is your most memorable
hockey experience?
**Winning gold with Cana-
da's Under-18 team in 2009**

What's something about yourself
that most people don't know?
**I'm funny and I like fool-
ing around with my older
brother, Ryan**

What is your favourite thing to do
on long bus rides?
**Listen to my iPod and
watch movies**

Who is your favourite superhero?
Batman

What is your favourite NHL team?
**The Dallas Stars and the
Florida Panthers**

Will he be dynamic offensively? Coach Wallin believes that Petrovic will be able to make the big shot from the point and that he has the ability to dictate the game from his end, not rushing his plays. To date, Alex is definitely able to skate the puck out of trouble, but he is certainly not considered to be a rushing offensive defenseman. Next year, with confidence and more time on the ice, Wallin is expecting that Petrovic will be the Rebels take-charge-with-the-puck player. He will be the quarterback for the team, making sure that the first pass is the right pass to make the play at the other end.

Alex played minor hockey in North Edmonton for the Eagles, North Stars, and Maple Leafs before making his debut into the world of Edmonton AAA. He participated in other sports like basketball and track and field, determined to do well in everything he tried. This determination plays out into his everyday life as well, and can be seen whether he was fixing his bike or studying for an exam in school. The Rebels are happy with his grades, and Alex is known as a good student.

Sometimes this determination bordered on perfectionism, especially when he was young, as everything had to be just right. Naturally, his parents worried about him when he was younger, feeling that he sometimes tried too hard to be perfect on the ice. This perfection, so far, has held him in good stead, as he is definitely one of the up-and-coming new and young talented hockey players.

In his 2008–09 season with the Red Deer Rebels, Alex was fifth among Red Deer defencemen for scoring, fourth among Red Deer rookies in scoring and second among Red Deer rookie defencemen in scoring. That year he was also named the Red Deer Rebels Rookie of the Year. Petrovic was also picked to be the assistant captain on Team Cherry in the 2010 CHL/NHL Home Hardware Top Prospects Game in Windsor, Ontario, where he picked up two assists to help lead his team to a 4–2 victory.

Hockey Canada saw this young prospect as being an asset to a few of their teams. At the 2009 World Under-17 Hockey Challenge in Port Alberni, Petrovic played for Team Pacific, helping them win a silver medal. He also attended the 2009 Men's National Under-18 Team Summer Selection Camp in August, cracked the final roster, giving him a ticket to the Czech Republic to earn a gold medal in the Memorial of Ivan Hlinka tournament. Although he wasn't chosen for Hockey Canada's Under-18 team in the spring, he will be looked at as a player who could make the IIHF World Junior team in the future, especially in 2012 when the Championship will be in Calgary/Edmonton and played on the smaller North American–style ice surface.

Alex Petrovic has a lot going for him and his journey into professional hockey will be watched by coaches, critics, and scouts across Canada. He is a tall kid, and many foresee that in the future he will create havoc on the blue line with his wicked shot and ability to take charge with the puck.

Petrovic was not invited to attend the Men's National Junior Team Summer Development Camp in August but he will be watched this fall as he plays for the Red Deer Rebels.

Petrovic has donned the Canada jersey with both the Under-17 program and for the summer Under-18 team.

Season	Event	Team	GP	G	A	Pts	+/-	PIM	
REGULAR SEASON									
2009–10	WHL	Red Deer Rebels	57	8	19	27	3	87	
2008–09	WHL	Red Deer Rebels	66	1	12	13	-4	70	
2007–08	WHL	Red Deer Rebels	10	1	0	1	0	2	
TOTALS			133	10	31	41	-1	159	
PLAYOFFS									
2010	WHL	Red Deer Rebels	4	0	0	0	-4	4	
TOTALS			4	0	0	0	-4	4	

Season	Event	Team	GP	G	A	PTS	+/-	PIM	
HOCKEY CANADA									
2009	Memorial of Ivan Hlinka	Under 18	4	0	0	0	–	2	Gold
2009	WU17HC	Pacific	6	2	1	3	–	4	Silver

Mark Pysyk

CANADA

Shoots: **Right**

Height: **6'1.5"**

Weight: **181 lbs**

Birthdate: **January 11, 1992**

Birthplace: **Edmonton, Alberta**

Hometown: **Sherwood Park, Alberta**

Team: **Edmonton Oil Kings, WHL**

MHA: **Strathcona MHA**

2010 NHL Entry Draft:
1st Round, 23rd Overall, Buffalo Sabres

In the Winter 2009–10 issue of the *Prospects Hockey* magazine, Mark Pysyk of the Edmonton Oil Kings was touted as the top WHL draft-eligible defenceman and the best in his age group. He was also given a big nod in *The Sporting News* and in many other scouting reports as being a top draft pick. Like a tennis ball, his name was bounced around all year, and he managed to keep the ball in the court as he ended up being the Buffalo Sabres' first selection to go in the 1st round, 23rd overall in the 2010 NHL Entry Draft. Added to his excellent draft ranking, Pysyk was also selected to attend the Men's National Junior Team Summer Development Camp in the hopes of winning a spot to play in the 2011 World Junior Championships, set to be in Buffalo, New York.

What is it about this young player that has the hockey world talking? According to the Oil Kings head coach, Steve Pleau, it is his explosive skating and his powerful initial three strides in any rush that make him such a dynamic player. Because Pysyk is able to get moving from stride one, he is able to effectively create separation from his opponents, allowing him to make some great plays. Pysyk is a player who can energize the rushes.

He is also a good size. Although he is not Chris Pronger huge, Pysyk has enough size, however, to be effective on the blue line. He stays extremely fit and is strong for his age. Maturity also goes a long way, and Pysyk is mature both on and off the ice. As a young player he has been able to log many

Pysyk as a young player in Strathcona, Alberta.

Mark playing for Team Pacific at the World Under-17 Hockey Challenge in 2009.

minutes for the Oil Kings, handling his ice time well. This has allowed him to play in varying situations and as a result he sees a lot of different hockey, giving him a good mind for the game. From his position on the blue line, he sees the ice, and sees the clear lanes to the net, giving him the opportunity to be one heck of a smart player when he hits the professional leagues.

All young players vying for that coveted position in the big leagues have things they need to improve on. Coach Pleau feels that having Mark continue to work on each of his shots—slapshot, snapshot, and wristshot—would be beneficial. To play good defence, a player has to have a quick shot. Pysyk continues to hone this skill with dedication and determination.

Mark grew up in Strathcona, Alberta, a rural area around Sherwood Park. He played for Strathcona in his early years then played his Midget AAA with the Sherwood Park Kings. Like many of the new hockey greats, Mark played other sports like soccer, volleyball, basketball, football, but it was hockey that he became passionate about. His parents remember the pivotal moment, when Mark realized hockey was his dream. They had taken him to an Edmonton Oilers game and, through friends, he got down to the Oilers locker room after the game. There he was introduced to Kevin Lowe and some of the Edmonton Oilers players. His eyes widened and he knew that one day he would like to become a professional hockey player.

Playing for the Strathcona Warriors Bantam AAA.

Pysyk is a strong player for the Edmonton Oil Kings.

Pysyk was selected in the 1st round, 3rd overall, by the Edmonton Oil Kings in the 2007 WHL bantam draft. In his first year of play he was eighth in Edmonton scoring, second among Edmonton defencemen in scoring, led Edmonton rookies in scoring, and was named the Edmonton Oil Kings Defenceman of the Year as well as Rookie of the Year. In the 2009–10 season, Pysyk took home some heavy hardware. He was awarded the Greg Tomalty Award as the Most Valuable Player, the Top Defenceman Award, and was the Scholastic Player of the Year. Mark was also selected to play for Team Orr, wearing an assistant captain letter, in the 2010 CHL/NHL Home Hardware Top Prospects Game. Taking all the accolades in stride, he is a player who sets goals and commits to achieving them.

His Hockey Canada debut was in 2009 when he played for Team Pacific at the World Under-17 Hockey Challenge in Port Alberni, winning a silver medal. In August of 2009, he attended the Men's National Under-18 Team Summer Selection Camp and after the evaluation process was named to the team that played in the Memorial of Ivan Hlinka tournament, winning the gold medal. Unfortunately, in the spring of 2010, he could have played in the IIHF World Under-18 Championship when the Oil Kings were knocked out of the playoffs, but he was still recovering from a broken foot.

Mark is a player with tremendous talent and potential to go far. He is a "Next One" to be watched—whether it is with the Edmonton Oil Kings, the Buffalo Sabres, or on Hockey Canada's National Junior Team.

SUMMER UPDATE

Pysyk attended the Men's National Under-18 Team Summer Selection Camp in August but only played in the first game for Team Red. He was sidelined in the second game for precautionary reasons due to a minor injury.

Pysyk protecting his goalie by taking the puck away from the shooter.

The Next Ones

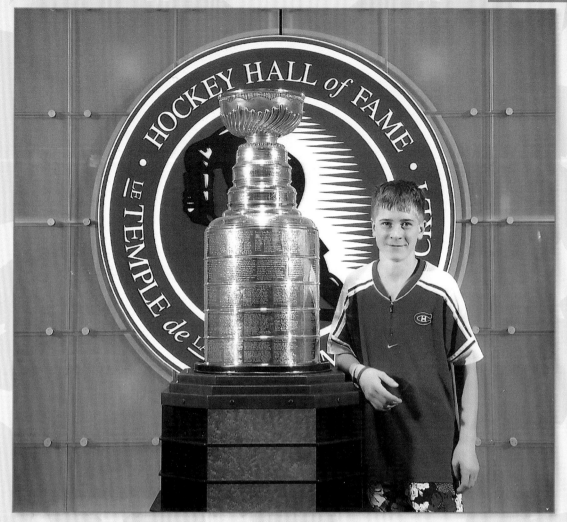

Age 11 at the Hockey Hall of Fame.

Season	Event	Team	GP	G	A	Pts	+/-	PIM	
		REGULAR SEASON							
2009–10	WHL	Edmonton Oil Kings	48	7	17	24	-19	47	
2008–09	WHL	Edmonton Oil Kings	61	5	15	20	-5	27	
2007–08	WHL	Edmonton Oil Kings	14	1	2	3	-8	8	
TOTALS			123	13	34	47	-32	82	
		PLAYOFFS							
2009	WHL	Edmonton Oil Kings	4	0	0	0	-9	2	
TOTALS			4	0	0	0	-9	2	
		HOCKEY CANADA							
Season	Event	Team	GP	G	A	PTS	+/-	PIM	
2009	Memorial of Ivan Hlinka	Under 18	4	0	2	2	–	2	Gold
2009	WU17HC	Pacific	6	1	3	4	–	6	Silver

Duncan Siemans

CANADA

Shoots: **Left**

Height: **6'3"**

Weight: **192 lbs**

Birthdate: **September 7, 1993**

Birthplace: **Edmonton, Alberta**

Hometown: **Sherwood Park, Alberta**

Team: **Saskatoon Blades, WHL**

MHA: **Sherwood Park MHA**

NHL Draft: **2011 Eligibility**

There must be something in Alberta's water; the boys seem to grow a bit bigger throughout the province. At the young age of sixteen, Duncan Siemans already stands an impressive 6'3". Only a few talented and fortunate players make major junior at sixteen, and for those that do, few actually see any ice time. Siemans, however, was given a unique opportunity for a young major junior player, earning a prominent role for the Saskatoon Blades in his first year in the WHL.

Not only did he play, he played a dominant role. Blades Head Coach, Lorne Molleken, used Siemans in every situation so Duncan could learn how to succeed in the really tough moments that come up in almost every game. This kid played on the penalty kill and the power play and logged some really heavy minutes.

Duncan is a big, strong kid who uses his size and strength to his advantage. For such a young player, this is a rare quality. Siemans played a smart game against twenty-year-old opponents with grit, power, and a solid presence. On the blue line he uses his good shot to get the puck close to the net. While this might suggest that Siemans is just a physical blue-line player, he also has an offensive upside to his play. A truly great skater, he has been known to rush the puck on occasion. With more experience and playing time, he will better learn how to read the rush, which will become an effective tool, helping take him to the

Duncan playing with the Sherwood Park Kings.

Look for Siemans to go high in the 2011 NHL Entry Draft.

Duncan Siemans

What is your favourite movie?
Never Back Down

What is your favourite
television show?
One Tree Hill

What is your favourite book?
The Outsiders

And your favourite magazine?
The Hockey News

What is your pre-game meal?
Pasta with ketchup

What is your favourite
family meal?
Chicken stir-fry

What is your favourite subject
in school?
Math

What is your favourite band?
Nickelback

What are your favourite activities
outside of hockey?
Camping, water sports,
quading, and paintball

Who is your hockey hero?
Scott Stevens

Who are your heroes outside
of hockey?
My family

What is your most memorable
hockey experience?
Winning the Western
Canadian Bantam Hockey
Championship

Tell us something about yourself
that most people don't know?
I'm quite shy until I get
to know people

What is your favourite thing to
do on long bus rides?
Sleep

Who is your favourite superhero?
Superman

What is your favourite NHL team?
The Edmonton Oilers,
I'm a hometown fan!

next level. Currently, his strong skating skills allow him to make up for any potential mistakes and enable him to skate out of trouble if needed.

Duncan grew up in Sherwood Park and played most of his minor hockey with the Sherwood Park Athletic Club (Kings) although he did play for Strathcona in his early years. He was a naturally gifted athlete from day one, and played soccer, baseball, volleyball, and football. He still holds school records in track and field and a provincial championship in football. For a short time he actually considered pursuing a future in football, though ultimately his love of hockey won.

The Blades picked Siemens as their number one choice in the WHL bantam draft in 2008. Siemens went 3rd overall in the 1st round and was the first defencemen picked by any team. Molleken has not been disappointed in his number one choice. At the end of his first season, Duncan was named the Saskatoon Blades Rookie of the Year.

Hockey Canada has also liked what they've seen in Siemens as he played for Team Pacific in the 2010 World Under-17 Hockey Challenge in Timmins, Ontario. And in June of 2010, he was invited to attend the 2010–11 Men's National Under-18 Team Summer Selection Camp which took place that August.

Born with innate athletic abilities, Siemens is gifted physically and has excelled in each sport he has competed in. At the age of three, he told his mother that he wanted his training wheels off his bike, went into the garage, and took them off himself. Wondering if he would fall, she watched him hop on his bike and ride it around and around in circles with no help from anyone. This natural balance has helped Siemans with his skating, making him a tremendous hockey player. His goals for next year with the Blades are to play a bigger role on the team, be more consistent, and defensively responsible.

This kid chose hockey over football and the hockey world is glad he did. Great things are around the corner for this big guy from Alberta.

Siemans was drafted as the Saskatoon Blades 1st pick in the 2008 WHL bantam draft.

Taking the before-game face-off at the 2010 World Under-17 Hockey Challenge. Siemans played for Team Pacific.

SUMMER UPDATE

Siemans played a strong tournament for the Summer U-18 Canadian Team, winning gold at the Memorial of Ivan Hlinka in the Czech Republic. Siemans picked up one goal and two assists for three points and ended with a +8.

Season	Event	Team	GP	G	A	Pts	+/-	PIM	
			REGULAR SEASON						
2009–10	WHL	Saskatoon Blades	57	3	17	20	11	89	
2008–09	WHL	Saskatoon Blades	2	0	1	1	2	2	
TOTALS			59	3	18	21	13	91	
			PLAYOFFS						
2010	WHL	Saskatoon Blades	7	0	0	0	1	11	
TOTALS			7	0	0	0	1	11	
			HOCKEY CANADA						
Season	Event	Team	GP	G	A	PTS	+/-	PIM	
2010	WU17HC	Pacific	5	0	0	0	–	10	4TH

Stephen Silas

CANADA

Shoots: **Left**

Height: **6'0.5"**

Weight: **188 lbs**

Birthdate: **June 26, 1992**

Birthplace: **Brampton, Ontario**

Hometown: **Georgetown, Ontario**

Team: **Belleville Bulls, OHL**

MHA: **Halton MHA**

2010 NHL Entry Draft:
4th Round, 95th Overall, Colorado Avalanche

When the Belleville Bulls had a fundraiser for the Military Resources Centre in Trenton, Ontario, Stephen Silas' Belleville Bulls jersey earned an incredible $7,500. Not bad for a seventeen-year-old hockey player who has yet to play a game in the NHL, or on an IIHF World Junior Team. But Silas does play strong for Belleville and that, combined with his solid performance on Canada's Under-18 Team, has made him a Canadian player to watch.

This young lad is an excellent, versatile skater. Like most young players his body is still filling out, but whatever size he doesn't have at the present time he makes up with smarts, good feet, and a strong stick.

Stephen started his hockey career in Georgetown, Ontario. From the very beginning, his natural instincts were to always guard and protect the puck. This automatic reaction slotted him as a defenceman, although he did move up and down the ice and out of position a bit as most young players do. At the age of eight, Silas started playing AAA. Like most young boys, Silas tried some other sports and found a secondary passion in lacrosse. In fact, he played on national peewee and bantam lacrosse teams and in his midget year was drafted 6th overall. His decision to play hockey or lacrosse wasn't a hard one to make, as Stephen always loved hockey more than lacrosse even though he wasn't drafted as high in hockey.

Silas was drafted by the Belleville Bulls as their first-round selection, 19th overall, in the 2008 OHL Priority Selection

A happy Stephen Silas playing minor hockey in Halton, Ontario.

Silas played for Team Ontario at the 2009 World
Under-17 Hockey Challenge and won a gold medal.

Stephen Silas

draft. In his first year with the Bulls he played big minutes, quite an accomplishment on a team full of veterans. Stephen fit right in with his strong mental game, allowing him to make some fairly significant contributions to the team. In the upcoming year, (2010–2011), the coach of the Bulls is anxious to see if Stephen will step up and respond as the quarterback, helping lead the squad. Having played for two years with extremely strong veteran defence, Stephen has always put himself as the second guy, but now he will be required to take charge.

Silas' stats have been good since he joined the Bulls. In the 2008–09 season, as a rookie, Silas was fourth in scoring for Bulls defence, second in scoring among Belleville rookies, and he led Belleville rookie defencemen in scoring. In his 2009–10 season, Stephen played in sixty-six games and earned forty-nine points, forty-five of which were assists. Such a number of helpers identifies what kind of a playmaker he is. He was also selected to play for Team Orr in the CHL/NHL Home Hardware Top Prospects Game in Windsor in January 2010. In the Home Hardware Skills Competition he placed second for Team Orr in the fastest-skater event.

Silas has been a big contributor in the Hockey Canada program. At the 2009 World Under-17 Hockey Challenge, Silas won a gold medal with Team Ontario. From there he was invited to the Men's National Under-18 Team Summer Selection Camp, making the team that would fly overseas to play in the 2009 Memorial of Ivan Hlinka tournament and winning gold. When the Belleville Bulls didn't make the playoffs in the spring of 2010, Silas was picked to play on the Under-18 team that travelled to Belarus to play in the IIHF World Under-18 Championship. Unfortunately, that team came back to Canada with a seventh place finish.

With lots of hard work on and off the ice, Stephen will naturally become a player who is ready to take the leap to the pros. He is a player with good skills, great skating, and who is known to work hard. He is dependable and constantly asks questions about how he can improve. Watch for him with the Belleville Bulls.

Silas (in white) crashing the net.

CANADA

SUMMER UPDATE

Silas did not attend the Men's National Junior Team Summer Development Camp in August but he is a player who will be watched over the next year.

Silas is a strong player for his OHL Team, the Belleville Bulls.

Season	Event	Team	GP	G	A	Pts	+/-	PIM	
REGULAR SEASON									
2009–10	OHL	Belleville Bulls	66	4	45	49	-27	61	
2008–09	OHL	Belleville Bulls	63	3	14	17	-2	18	
TOTALS			129	7	59	66	-29	79	
PLAYOFFS									
2009	OHL	Belleville Bulls	17	0	0	0	-3	10	
TOTALS			17	0	0	0	-3	10	
HOCKEY CANADA									
Season	Event		Team	GP	G	A	PTS	+/-	PIM	
2010	IIHF World Under-18 World Championship		Under 18	6	0	2	2	–	0	7th
2009	Memorial of Ivan Hlinka		Under 18	4	0	1	–	1	2	Gold
2009	WU17HC		Ontario	6	1	7	8	–	2	Gold

Stephen Silas

Brett Connolly

Shoots: **Right**

Height: **6'2"**

Weight: **184 lbs**

Birthdate: **May 2, 1992**

Birthplace: **Campbell River, British Columbia**

Hometown: **Prince George, British Columbia**

Team: **Prince George Cougars, WHL**

MHA: **Prince George MHA**

2010 NHL Entry Draft:
1st Round, 6th Overall, Tampa Bay Lightning

Even though Brett Connolly was injured for a good part of the 2009–10 season, playing only sixteen games for the Prince George Cougars of the WHL, he was still drafted in the 2010 NHL Entry Draft in the 1st round, 6th overall by Tampa Bay Lightning. Now that says something about this young man and his talent as a hockey player. Obviously, Tampa Bay's General Manager, Steve Yzerman, was able to look beyond the current injury and Brett's shortened season, making some good, solid predictions that this kid was worth the risk.

The hip injury started at the 2009 Memorial of Ivan Hlinka in the Czech Republic, and although Connolly made a valiant effort to start his year with the Cougars, he found himself hurting his hip again, knowing that the only thing that would help him would be rehabilitation and rest. In December, he came back for five games to finish off 2009, but when it came time for the CHL/NHL Home Hardware Top Prospects Game in 2010, his injury forced him to bow out.

So what is it about Connolly that has made everyone look past his injury? Most will say it is because he is "that" player. When he gets the puck, people sit on the edge of their seat just to see what he is going to do. With Prince George, in their regular season, he came back for the last few games, and although he had been out for most of the season, he lit a fire under his team and created a tremendous amount of tension on the ice, especially when the team played their last two road games.

Brett learning how to skate at a very early age.

Connolly is a strong skater for
the Prince George Cougars.

What is your favourite movie?
The Blindside

What is your favourite television show?
Two and a Half Men

What is your favourite book?
Playing with Fire
by Theo Fleury

And your favourite magazine?
Sports Illustrated

What is your pre-game meal?
Pasta with meat sauce

What is your favourite family meal?
Steak

What is your favourite subject in school?
English

What is your favourite band?
Nickelback

What are your favourite activities outside of hockey?
Swimming, tubing, and golfing

Who is your hockey hero?
Sidney Crosby

Who is your hero outside of a hockey?
Terry Fox

What is your most memorable hockey experience?
Winning CHL Rookie of the Year

What's something about yourself that most people don't know?
In 2009, I had a day named after me: Brent Connolly Day

What are your favourite things to do on long bus rides?
Sleep, watch movies, listen to music

Who is your favourite superhero?
Superman

What is your favourite NHL team?
The Pittsburgh Penguins and the Tampa Bay Lightning

Offensively gifted with fantastic hands, he is also a solid skater, which is a lethal combination in a forward. His coach in Prince George, Dean Clark, says he just has "that nose for the net" and "you know when he's on the ice something can happen." Connolly is also known to enhance the play of his teammates when they share the ice. Some players make themselves better but Connolly has that rare gift of boosting other players. He is a good on-ice leader. He's not the most verbose kid, and he probably wouldn't be labelled as a big talker, but when he does have something to say it is well meant and gets the attention of his teammates.

Connolly started playing minor hockey in Port Hardy, but in 2002 his family moved to Prince George and he played the rest of his minor hockey and WHL in northern British Columbia. He stayed at home for the draft, (Prince George drafted him as their 1st round selection, 10th overall in the 2007 WHL bantam draft), and has the convenience of being four minutes from the rink, an option that not many major junior players have, as most are billeted away from home. In his first year with the Cougars, he won Prince George's MVP and rookie of the year awards, leading Prince George in goals and points, and Prince George rookies in goals, assists, and points. He led all WHL rookies in goals and was

Connolly (white # 12) getting ready to score with Team Pacific at the 2009 World Under-17 Hockey Challenge.

(*left*) Connolly was the CHL Rookie of the Year in 2008/09.

Brett Connolly

named WHL rookie of the year and CHL rookie of the year for the 2008–09 season.

Two years running, Connolly has played in the IIHF World Under-18 Championship, finishing fourth in 2009 in Fargo, North Dakota and seventh in 2010 in Belarus. He graced the ice in 2009 with Team Pacific at the 2009 World Under-17 Hockey Challenge in Port Alberni, winning a silver medal. And, of course, he played in the 2009 Memorial of Ivan Hlinka tournament in the Czech Republic, which was where he sustained his hip injury. Connolly's name was left off the Men's National Junior Team Summer Development Camp roster for the summer of 2010, but that doesn't mean you won't see this player on the team come Christmas. So much depends on his start in the fall of 2010 and his injury level. More games on the ice will help Connolly's chances.

Connolly is a gifted forward who, like every young forward, is working on his defensive play. He trains hard and has no intention of letting an injury get in his way. Hopefully, this young player will see a full season next year instead of just sixteen games so he can push people to the edge of their seats and show the hockey world what he can really do.

SUMMER UPDATE

Although Connolly was not invited to the Men's National Junior Team Summer Development Camp he is a player the scouts will watch with interest this fall as he plays for the Prince George Cougars.

Connolly has been a strong member of many Hockey Canada teams and played in two IIHF World Under-18 Championships.

Connolly is gifted with fantastic hands and strong skating skills.

Season	Event	Team	GP	G	A	Pts	+/-	PIM	
REGULAR SEASON									
2009–10	WHL	Prince George Cougars	16	10	9	19	-3	8	
2008–09	WHL	Prince George Cougars	65	30	30	60	-26	38	
2007–08	WHL	Prince George Cougars	4	0	0	0	-3	0	
TOTALS			85	40	39	79	-32	46	
PLAYOFFS									
2009	WHL	Prince George Cougars	4	0	2	2	-2	6	
TOTALS	WHL	Prince George Cougars	4	0	2	2	-2	6	
HOCKEY CANADA									
Season	Event	Team	GP	G	A	PTS	+/-	PIM	
2010	IIHF World Under-18 Championship	Under 18	4	1	0	1	–	0	7th
2009	Memorial of Ivan Hlinka	Under 18	2	0	1	1	–	0	Gold
2009	IIHF World Under-18 Championship	Under 18	6	3	3	6	–	4	4th
2009	WU17HC	Pacific	6	3	5	8	–	2	Silver

Brett Connolly

Sean Couturier

CANADA

Shoots: **Left**

Height: **6'3"**

Weight: **185 lbs**

Birthdate: **December 7, 1992**

Birthplace: **Phoenix, Arizona**

Hometown: **Bathurst, New Brunswick**

Team: **Drummondville Voltigeurs, QMJHL**

MHA: **Bathurst MHA**

NHL Draft: **2011 Eligibility**

Look for 6'3", 185 lbs Sean Couturier in the 2011 draft even though he is from the 1992 birth year. With a December birthday, this Drummondville Voltigeurs forward will have a good chance of being ranked high when it comes to his draft year if he keeps playing well and improving his game. His size alone sets him apart, not to mention his offensive talents.

Couturier was born in Phoenix, Arizona when his father, Sylvain Couturier, was playing for the Phoenix Roadrunners of the IHL. When Sean was old enough to start playing organized hockey, his family moved to Germany because Sean's father had secured a spot on the Berlin Capitals. Sean started his early, minor hockey career playing in Germany and when his family did return to Canada, he played novice and atom in Quebec. Then his father took a job with the Acadie-Bathurst team, and Sean played three years of peewee and one year of bantam in Bathurst, followed by one year of midget with the Miramichi Rivermen where he was named the New Brunswick Major Midget Hockey League Rookie of the Year in 2007. Then it was time for Sean to move again—only this time he packed his bags and left without his parents. He took the big step to leave home and attend Notre Dame in Saskatchewan. The change was difficult at first, but Sean adapted quite quickly to playing on the coveted AAA Midget Hounds, and that year his team won the Saskatchewan Midget AAA Hockey League championship.

Although Sean started playing minor hockey in Germany, he has lots of experience with Hockey Canada.

The Next Ones

Big smiles for Couturier after winning the
Memorial of Ivan Hlinka in 2009.

Q & A

What is your favourite movie?
Slap Shot

What is your favourite television show?
The Simpsons

What is your favourite magazine?
The Hockey News

What is your pre-game meal?
Chicken and pasta

What is your favourite family meal?
Chinese Fondue

What is your favourite subject in school?
Math

What is your favourite band?
Red Hot Chili Peppers

What is your favourite activity outside of hockey?
Tennis

Who is your hockey hero?
Evgeni Malkin

Who is your hero outside of hockey?
Tom Brady

What is your most memorable hockey experience?
Playing in the Memorial Cup in Rimouski

What's something about yourself that most people don't know?
I lived in Germany as a child and used to speak German fluently

What is your favourite thing to do on long bus rides
Watch movies

What is your favourite NHL team?
The New Jersey Devils

Getting back to his family on the East Coast didn't take long, when, at the 2008 QMJHL entry draft, Drummondville selected Sean as their first-round choice, making him the 2nd overall draft pick. In his first year in the QMJHL, Sean got the opportunity to go to the Memorial Cup after the Voltigeurs won the Presidents Cup, earning them a berth. At the Memorial Cup tournament, the Voltigeurs managed to make it to the semifinal, only to lose to Windsor 3–2 in overtime. By the end of this first year, Sean had secured a regular spot on the first line and was second among scoring among Drummondville rookies.

In his second year with Drummondville, Sean stepped up to take on a more sophomore role and finished off his season leading the QMJHL league in scoring and with his team making it to the third round of the run for the QMJHL President's Cup. Unfortunately, they were beaten by the Moncton Wildcats in the semifinals. At the QMJHL Golden Pucks awards banquet in the spring of 2010, Couturier won the Trophée Jean Beliveau (meilleur marqueur de la sasion), the top-scorer award. In regular season play he had ninety-six points, with fifty-five assists and forty-one goals.

Couturier's Junior career has been with the Drummondville Voltigeurs.

Couturier could go high in the 2011 NHL Entry Draft if he has a good season with Drummondville.

Sean Couturier

CANADA

One of Sean's dreams was to wear the red and white Hockey Canada jersey, and he has certainly had an opportunity to realize that dream. He played two years in the Under-17 program. In 2008 he played with Team Atlantic at the World Under-17 Hockey Challenge in London, Ontario finishing eighth, and in 2009 he played with the same team in Port Alberni, where his team finished ninth. Sean was also a member of the 2009 Under-18 Summer Team that travelled to the Czech Republic for the Memorial of Ivan Hlinka tournament, winning a gold medal. Sean would have been a contender for the Under-18 team in 2010, but with Drummondville making it to the Presidents Cup semifinals, playing wasn't an option. In the spring of 2010, Couturier was invited to attend the Men's National Junior Team Summer Development Camp in August.

Sean Couturier is a solid forward who has made great strides with the Drummondville Voltigeurs. Look for him to be one of the top picks in the 2011 Entry Draft if he keeps on playing up to his potential.

Sean played two years in Hockey Canada's U-17 program as well as playing Under-18.

The Next Ones

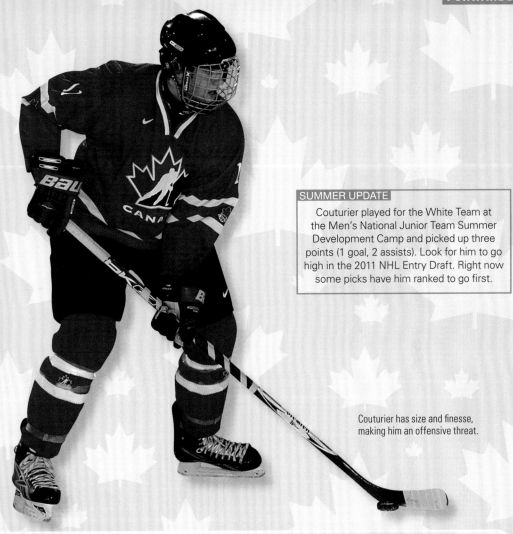

SUMMER UPDATE

Couturier played for the White Team at the Men's National Junior Team Summer Development Camp and picked up three points (1 goal, 2 assists). Look for him to go high in the 2011 NHL Entry Draft. Right now some picks have him ranked to go first.

Couturier has size and finesse, making him an offensive threat.

Season	Event	Team	GP	G	A	Pts	+/-	PIM	
REGULAR SEASON									
2009–10	QMJHL	Drummondville Voltigeurs	68	41	55	96	62	47	
2008–09	QMJHL	Drummondville Voltigeurs	58	9	22	31	24	14	
TOTALS			126	50	77	127	86	61	
PLAYOFFS									
2010	QMJHL	Drummondville Voltigeurs	14	10	8	18	11	18	
2009	QMJHL	Drummondville Voltigeurs	19	1	7	8	-1	8	
TOTALS			33	11	15	26	10	26	
HOCKEY CANADA									
Season	Event	Team	GP	G	A	PTS	+/-	PIM	
2009	Memorial of Ivan Hlinka	Under 18	4	1	1	2	–	2	Gold
2009	WU17HC	Atlantic	5	5	4	9	–	4	9th
2008	WU17HC	Atlantic	5	0	1	1	–	2	8th

Sean Couturier

Brendan Gallagher

CANADA

Shoots: **Right**

Height: **5'8"**

Weight: **163 lbs**

Birthdate: **June 5, 1992**

Birthplace: **Delta, British Columbia**

Hometown: **Edmonton, Alberta**

Team: **Vancouver Giants, WHL**

MHA: **Greater Vancouver Canadians**

2010 NHL Entry Draft:
5th Round, 147th Overall, Montreal Canadiens

A relentless checker, Brendan Gallagher possesses the style of play that could allow him to fit quite nicely into a Hockey Canada lineup, especially at the World Junior level. What he lacks in size, he makes up for in competitiveness. He is known in hockey circles as the guy that never gives up. He keeps playing no matter what odds are stacked against him, and will continue to chase the puck until the horn signals the end of the game. Brendan only stands at 5'8"—short by professional hockey standards. Had he been 6'0" during his Draft year, NHL teams might have been more apt to snap him up. As it was, Gallagher's name was left off the NHL Combine List, and at the 2010 NHL Entry Draft in Los Angeles he went in the 5th round, 147th overall to the Montreal Canadiens. Still, no one can dispute the fact that in his 2009–10 season with the WHL Vancouver Giants, Gallagher scored forty-one goals and picked up forty assists for a total of eighty-one points, leading the Giants in goals scored for the season. Then in sixteen playoff games he managed an impressive eleven goals and ten assists, earning yet another twenty-one points. It should be noted that in Gallagher's 2009–10 season with the Giants he racked up a hefty 111 penalty minutes.

His consistent, hard play and points tally may have been lost by the various NHL scouts and their teams, but it certainly piqued the interest of Hockey Canada. They knew better than to leave this super-competitive player off the Men's National Junior

Gallagher started his minor hockey career in Edmonton before moving to Vancouver.

Gallagher has enjoyed tremendous success with the Vancouver Giants.

Brendan Gallagher

Q & A

What is your favourite movie?
Step Brothers

What is your favourite television show?
The Office

What is your favourite book?
Muhammad Ali's autobiography.

And your favourite magazine?
The Hockey News

What is your pre-game meal?
Chicken, pasta, and salad

What is your favourite family meal?
Steak and potatoes

What is your favourite subject in school?
Biology

What is your favourite band?
Nickelback

What is your favourite activity outside of hockey?
Golf

Who is your hockey hero?
Martin St. Louis

Who is your hero outside of hockey?
Steve Nash

What is your most memorable hockey experience?
Winning three provincial championships in minor hockey

What's something about yourself that most people don't know?
I skipped the seventh grade

What is your favourite thing to do on long bus rides?
Watch movies

Who is your favourite superhero?
Batman

What is your favourite NHL team?
The Montreal Canadiens

Team Summer Development Camp list. They liked his speed, his puck protection, play-making, and scoring ability, but almost more importantly, they were impressed with his voracious appetite for making and finishing a check.

Although Gallagher calls Vancouver home, he started his minor hockey career in Edmonton with Sherwood Park. In his second year of peewee hockey, the Gallagher family moved to Tsawwassen, British Columbia, an area just south of Vancouver, though Brendan played some forty-five minutes away at the Burnaby Winter Club because he had a friend who encouraged him to sign up for the team. The next year, and much closer to home, Gallagher played with the South Delta Minor Hockey Association.

In the 2007 WHL bantam draft, while he was still with South Delta, Gallagher was a 9th round selection, (195th overall), by the Vancouver Giants. After his bantam draft year, Brendan played a year with the Vancouver Canadians of the BC Major Midget League, and his team came in second in BCMML standings. Gallagher led his team in scoring, and in thirty-nine games notched twenty-three goals and thirty-three assists for a total of fifty-six points. His team ended up losing to the Okanagan Rockets in the semifinals of the playoffs. Having a good major midget season helped Gallagher make the jump to the WHL and the Vancouver Giants when he was just sixteen years old. In his first season with the Giants, in fifty-two games, he scored ten goals, and recorded another twenty-six assists.

It was in 2008 that Hockey Canada first noticed this tenacious, undersized forward. Gallagher played for Team Pacific at the 2009 World Under-17 Hockey Challenge in Port Alberni, playing all six games, scoring two goals, and adding three assists for a total of five points. But it wasn't Gallagher's points that everyone talked about—although they certainly upped his ante—it was the relentless checking from such a small guy that became the hot topic. Even so, Gallagher did face a big disappointment when he wasn't selected to play on the Men's National Under-18 Team. Sometimes big letdowns make a player work that much harder, and Gallagher didn't waste his time dwelling on the loss but instead continued showing up to play hard for his WHL team and to show the hockey world what he could do.

Multi-point games, hard hits to his opponents, and fierce competitiveness are but some of the words used to describe Brendan Gallagher. His size is arguable, but his production and level of play aren't.

SUMMER UPDATE

Small but mighty, Gallagher picked up one assist when he played for Team White at the Men's National Junior Team Summer Development Camp

Gallagher played for Team Pacific at the 2009 World Under-17 Hockey Challenge.

Season	Event	Team	GP	G	A	Pts	+/-	PIM	
REGULAR SEASON									
2009–10	WHL	Vancouver Giants	72	41	40	81	9	111	
2008–09	WHL	Vancouver Giants	52	10	21	31	26	61	
TOTALS			124	51	61	112	35	172	
PLAYOFFS									
2010	WHL	Vancouver Giants	16	11	10	21	10	14	
2009	WHL	Vancouver Giants	16	1	2	3	-2	10	
TOTALS			32	12	12	24	8	24	

	HOCKEY CANADA								
Season	Event	Team	GP	G	A	PTS	+/-	PIM	
2009	WU17HC	Pacific	6	2	3	5	–	12	Silver

Brendan Gallagher

Taylor Hall

CANADA

Shoots: **Left**

Height: **6'0"**

Weight: **185 lbs**

Birthdate: **November 14, 1991**

Birthplace: **Calgary, Alberta**

Hometown: **Kingston, Ontario**

MHA: **Kingston MHA**

Team: **Windsor Spitfires, OHL**

2010 NHL Entry Draft:
1st Round, 1st Overall, Edmonton Oilers

Anyone who knows anything about hockey knows that Taylor Hall is *the* young Canadian player to watch. His hockey resumé is almost as long as Santa's naughty and nice list. It's complete with two Memorial Cup victories, a silver medal from the IIHF World Junior Championship, gold medals for Hockey Canada in the IIHF World Under-18 Championships and at the Memorial of Ivan Hlinka Under-18 tournament, and many, many awards. And, of course, most recently he earned his rightful place in history when he was selected 1st in the 2010 NHL Entry Draft. For most of the 2009–2010 hockey season Taylor Hall's name could be heard almost everywhere. One week he was slotted as the number-one NHL Draft pick and the next week he was number two. On the odd occasion, his name slipped to three, but those times were few and far between. In the end, Edmonton Oilers General Manager, Steve Tambellini ended the debate and selected Taylor with his team's cherished first overall 1st round, number-one Draft pick.

Hall is one of those very special, rare players that makes an impact each time he enters a dressing room, joins a bench, or steps onto the ice. Fans and scouts are lifted from their seats when he gets the puck—anticipating that he will develop a spectacular play. All eyes were on him when he played for Hockey Canada on the 2010 IIHF World Junior Team; he didn't disappoint. Even at the young age of eighteen, he scored six goals and gathered six assists.

Taylor started his hockey career in Calgary with Nasa and McKnight before his family moved to Kingston.

The Next Ones

Hall was a force when he played in the 2010 World Junior Championship in Saskatoon.

Q & A

Taylor also helped his team, the Windsor Spitfires, win the MasterCard Memorial Cup two years in a row, and became the first player to ever win the MVP award twice, collecting the Stafford Smythe Trophy at the 2009 event in Rimouski, Quebec as well as in 2010 in Brandon, Manitoba. He also led the 2010 tournament in scoring with nine points in four games while scoring a tournament high of five goals. In the final game, where Windsor met with the Brandon Wheat Kings, Hall scored a goal and claimed two assists to help his team win 9–1.

Taylor is an only child. His father was an athlete, having played in the CFL and was also on the Canadian bobsled team as a pusher and a braker. Taylor grew up in the world of competition, going to the track with his father. Born with a natural competitive drive, he learned about competition by watching his father.

Calgary was Taylor's first minor hockey home and he started off playing for Nasa and McKnight. Then his family moved to Kingston, where Taylor played midget hockey, starting off in minor midget; his team won the Ottawa district and OHL Cup.

At the age of fifteen (he has a late November birthday), Taylor left home to play for the Windsor Spitfires. They had drafted him as their 1st selection, 2nd overall in the 2007 OHL Priority Selection draft. That year he ended up third in scoring for Windsor, led the team in goals, led the rookies in scoring, was second among all OHL rookies in scoring, and 18th in OHL scoring. He also was selected to play for the OHL in the 2010 ADT Canada-Russia Challenge. In his second year in the OHL, Hall earned many player-of-the-week awards and continued on his scoring warpath. One of his big accomplishments that season was helping the Spitfires win the OHL playoffs, where he was named the MVP after he recorded a lofty thirty-six points in twenty games.

For Hockey Canada, Taylor has played for numerous teams. As well as playing in an IIHF World Junior Championship, he graced the ice for the 2008 Memorial of Ivan Hlinka tournament and the 2007–2008 IIHF World Under-18 Championship, winning gold in both tournaments. He was the third top scorer for Canada at the IIHF World Championships and he was tied for first in scoring at the 2008 Memorial of Ivan Hlinka. Hall also played for Team Ontario in 2006 in the World Under-17 Hockey Challenge where he picked up his first gold medal. Of course, he was invited to attend the Men's National Junior Team Summer Development Camp in the summer of 2010, and whether he plays for Team Canada at Christmas 2010 will depend on his first few months with the Edmonton Oilers. The Oilers might not release him to play in the 2011 World Junior Championship in Buffalo but chances are he will wear the red and white jersey in the future.

Hall took his OHL Team, the Windsor Spitfires,
to the MasterCard Memorial Cup two years running.

Taylor Hall

CANADA

There is no doubt that Taylor Hall is an extremely talented hockey player. His passion for scoring is incredible, and his ability to anticipate the play always leads him to the right offensive spot at the right time. A fantastic skater, he moves to the outside with great speed, pushing past players to get to the net. At full speed, he is willing to take a hit. Taylor has a willingness to pay the price if it means he can create a scoring chance, and he has no fear of going to the tough areas and mixing it up in the corners. While his offensive skills are natural and polished, he also continues to work on his defensive play to become a better all-around player.

Taylor Hall is *the* next one to watch.

Winning a silver medal at the 2010 World Junior Championship in Saskatoon.

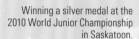
SUMMER UPDATE

Although invited to the Men's National Junior Team Summer Development Camp, Hall did not attend because of his commitment to the Edmonton Oilers.

Hall is a tough player who isn't afraid to go to tough areas.

Season	Event	Team	GP	G	A	Pts	+/-	PIM	
REGULAR SEASON									
2009–10	OHL	Windsor Spitfires	57	40	66	106	46	56	
2008–09	OHL	Windsor Spitfires	63	38	52	90	29	60	
2007–08	OHL	Windsor Spitfires	63	45	39	84	40	22	
TOTALS			183	123	157	280	115	138	
PLAYOFFS									
2009	OHL	Windsor Spitfires	20	16	20	36	15	12	
2008	OHL	Windsor Spitfires	5	2	3	5	-6	2	
HOCKEY CANADA									
Season	Event	Team	GP	G	A	PTS	+/-	PIM	
2010	IIHF World Junior Championship	Under 20	6	6	6	12	–	0	Silver
2008	Memorial of Ivan Hlinka	Under 18	4	2	4	6	–	2	Gold
2008	IIHF World Under-18 Championship	Under 18	7	4	5	9	–	4	Gold
2006	WU17HC	Ontario	5	4	4	8	–	4	Gold

Taylor Hall

Curtis Hamilton

CANADA

Shoots: **Left**

Height: **6'2"**

Weight: **211 lbs**

Birthdate: **December 4, 1991**

Birthplace: **Tacoma, Washington USA**

Hometown: **Kelowna, British Columbia**

Team: **Saskatoon Blades, WHL**

MHA: **Kelowna MHA**

2010 NHL Entry Draft:
2nd Round, 48th Overall, Edmonton Oilers

This young man has been hanging around arenas watching major junior hockey since he was born, and by the way Curtis Hamilton plays, he obviously picked up a thing or two along the way. At the 2010 NHL Entry Draft, Hamilton went in the 2nd round, 48th overall to the Edmonton Oilers. This came after a season where he had been plagued with injuries, having played in only twenty-six games. He was also on the invitation list to attend the Men's National Junior Team Summer Development Camp.

Curtis Hamilton's father, Bruce Hamilton, is the General Manager of the Kelowna Rockets, and young Curtis spent considerable time trailing after his father and watching WHL hockey. Curtis was born during the Rockets inaugural season, when the team still played in the big Tacoma Dome in Washington. On game days, Curtis would put his skates on in the house and play hockey with his nervous cat as the goalie and a table tennis ball as the puck. In 1995, the Rockets new owner moved the team to Kelowna, and the Hamilton family followed. It was then that Curtis first started playing hockey on a team.

He excelled right away, playing minor hockey in Kelowna, but when he hit his teens he moved on to play rep hockey (or as many in the Okanagan would say), he played on "the travelling team." He played for the Okanagan Rockets of the BC Major Midget League.

Curtis grew quickly and when the WHL bantam draft rolled around, even with a late December birthday, he impressed the

Curtis began playing minor hockey in Kelowna.

Hamilton has been a strong player in the WHL.

Curtis Hamilton

What is your favourite movie?
Friday Night Lights

What is your favourite
television show?
Seinfeld

What is your favourite book?
The Lord of the Rings

And your favourite magazine?
The Hockey News

What is your pre-game meal?
Pasta and chicken

What is your favourite
family meal?
Greek ribs, lemon rice,
and veggies

What is your favourite subject
in school?
History

What is your favourite activity
outside of hockey?
Hanging out with friends

Who is your hockey hero?
Wayne Gretzky

Who is your hero outside
of hockey?
My dad

What is your most memorable
hockey experience?
Playing at the World
Under-18 Championship

What's something about yourself
that most people don't know?
I'm very good at table tennis

What is your favourite thing
to do on long bus rides?
Sleep and play cards

Who is your favourite superhero?
Batman

scouts with his size and strength. The Saskatoon Blades picked him up in the 2nd round of the 2006 WHL bantam draft (36th overall) and at the young age of fifteen, he made the move from Kelowna to Saskatoon, making his debut on October 20, 2006.

By the end of his first year, he was playing on the second line as a winger. His size certainly helped his game, but he is a big kid with tremendous hockey sense. He reads the game well and has developed into a well-rounded player, working effectively in both the offensive and the defensive zone. Playing the tough areas is not an issue for Curtis, and he uses his size when necessary. His coach with the Blades, Lorne Molleken, has used Curtis on the penalty kill and has slotted him as a top unit on the power play.

Unfortunately for Curtis, injuries ruined most of his 2009–2010 season. Two collarbone injuries and a knee injury sidelined him for much of the season. He worked hard off the ice to speed up the healing process, and managed to get back on the ice during the post-season. The Blades won their first round against the Red Deer Rebels in a four-game sweep, but fell to the Brandon Wheat Kings in the second round.

In 2009, Hamilton made his debut with Hockey Canada when he played at the 2009 IIHF World Under-18 Hockey Championships in North Dakota and Minnesota. Canada finished in fourth place, losing the bronze medal to Finland in a shootout.

Injury free, Curtis Hamilton could be a tremendous asset to Hockey Canada and the professional world of hockey. He has size and skill and isn't afraid to use these attributes. Nor is he adverse to setbacks, never letting his frustration get the better of his training, and acknowledging that hard work is what it takes to come back from an injury. Every day he tries to do something better and that is what makes a great hockey player.

Currently, he is working on his overall quickness and his first few steps, hoping that with this extra skill set he will get to the next level, the pros.

Hamilton started with the Blades
at the age of fifteen.

Erik

Hamilton uses his size to his advantage.

SUMMER UPDATE

Hamilton played on Team Red at the Men's National Junior Team Summer Development Camp in August, picking up an assist in the second game. Red lost both games.

CANADA

Season	Event	Team	GP	G	A	Pts	+/-	PIM	
REGULAR SEASON									
2009–10	WHL	Saskatoon Blades	26	7	9	16	9	6	
2008–09	WHL	Saskatoon Blades	58	20	28	48	28	24	
2007–08	WHL	Saskatoon Blades	68	14	13	27	-15	43	
2006–07	WHL	Saskatoon Blades	2	0	0	0	-2	0	
TOTALS			154	41	50	91	20	73	
PLAYOFFS									
2010	WHL	Saskatoon Blades	5	2	1	3	4	6	
2009	WHL	Saskatoon Blades	7	1	1	2	0	2	
TOTALS			12	3	2	5	4	8	
HOCKEY CANADA									
Season	Event	Team	GP	G	A	PTS	+/-	PIM	
2009	IIHF World Under-18 Championship	Under 18	6	1	4	5	–	4	4th

Curtis Hamilton

Quinton Howden

CANADA

Shoots: **Left**

Height: **6'2.5"**

Weight: **185 lbs**

Birthdate: **January 21, 1992**

Birthplace: **Winnipeg, Manitoba**

Hometown: **Oakbank, Manitoba**

MHA: **Springfield MHA**

Team: **Moose Jaw Warriors, WHL**

2010 NHL Entry Draft:
1st Round, 25th Overall, Florida Panthers

The eldest of four, Quinton Howden does exhibit some of the "oldest child" birth order characteristics—the most obvious being his perfectionism. Of course, for a hockey player, this can be a good trait, as he is extremely hard-working, is always well-prepared, and has shown that he can be a professional player at the age of seventeen.

Quinton is known for his size and speed, which makes him an up-and-coming power forward. Those traits coupled with his good shot and great mental focus make him a real competitor, a player who always wants to win. This young player came into Moose Jaw from a team where he was considered the best player on the ice. In his first year with the WHL, Howden had to adapt to playing a different role, and he found a challenge in being one of many talented players. But he figured out what he had to do, and as well as being an offensive threat, he turned himself into a shut-down checking player, giving him the opportunity to play more than one role. Now he definitely sticks his nose into piles and as time progresses, with his mental ability sure to improve, he will do that more consistently, making him an extremely challenging and frustrating opponent. He sometimes forgets that he is a kid, because he is always thinking about his game and what he needs to do to improve.

Cochrane, Alberta was his first hockey home, and he played there until he was twelve. When Quinton was in Grade 6, the Howden family moved to Winnipeg and he started playing with

Quinton began playing minor hockey in Cochrane, Alberta.

The Next Ones

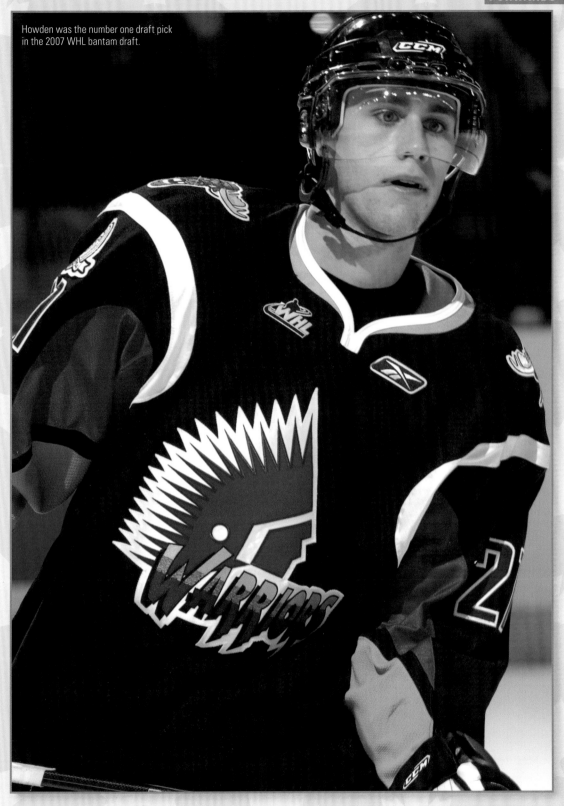

Howden was the number one draft pick in the 2007 WHL bantam draft.

What are your favourite movies?
Bad Boys 2, Never Back Down,
and *Gone in 60 Seconds*

What is your favourite
television show?
Friends

What is your favourite book?
Mind Gym

And your favourite magazine?
The Hockey News

What is your pre-game meal?
Chicken and pasta with
alfredo sauce

What is your favourite
family meal?
Steak and lobster

What are your favourite subjects
in school?
Math and sciences

What is your favourite band?
Nickelback

What are your favourite activities
outside of hockey?
Golf, snowmobiling, and
water sports

Who is your hockey hero?
Sidney Crosby

Who are your heroes outside
of hockey?
My dad and brother

What are your most memorable
hockey experiences?
Getting drafted to the
WHL and winning gold
at the Ivan Hlinka
tournament

What's something about yourself
that most people don't know?
I broke my femur when
I was five

What are your favourite things to
do on long bus rides?
Hang out with the guys
and watch movies

Who is your favourite superhero?
Batman

What is your favourite NHL team?
The Calgary Flames and
the Florida Panthers

the Oakbank Minor Hockey Association and then the Springfield Minor Hockey Association. In 2006, when Howden was playing peewee, his Springfield Icehawks won gold at the Manitoba provincial championships, and in 2007 his Springfield bantam team made it to the provincial semifinals. In his 2004–05 peewee season Quinton racked up more than three hundred points!

When the 2007 WHL draft rolled around, the Moose Jaw Warriors were slotted to have the first overall pick and they didn't hesitate to select Manitoba boy, Quinton Howden. He had definitely caught the eyes of the scouts. In his first full season (2008–09) with the Warriors, he was ninth in Moose Jaw scoring and he led all Moose Jaw rookies in goals, assists, and total points. That year he was named Moose Jaw Rookie of the Year.

In the 2009–10 season, Quinton has kept climbing and progressing in the WHL. In January of 2010 he was selected to play in the CHL/NHL Home Hardware Top Prospects Game, and was slotted on Team Orr. During the skills competition, Howden made his mark when he won the shooting accuracy event in a sudden death tiebreaker. At the end of the 2009–10 WHL season, in sixty-five games, Howden had scored twenty-eight goals and thirty-seven assists for a total of sixty-five points. He was the top scorer for the Moose Jaw Warriors.

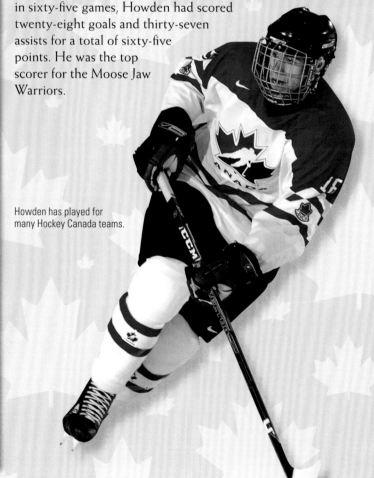

Howden has played for many Hockey Canada teams.

Howden is known for his size and speed.

Quinton Howden

Hockey Canada has also been a fan of Quinton Howden. In the 2009 World Under-17 Hockey Challenge, Howden played for Team West, finishing fourth. Obviously, he made an impression on the scouts because he was selected to attend the Men's National Under-18 Team Summer Selection Camp in Calgary that August. At the end of the camp, Howden was asked to play for Canada in the 2009 Memorial of Ivan Hlinka tournament. And, in the spring of 2010, Howden was one of seven players from the WHL selected to play for Canada at the 2010 IIHF World Under-18 Championship in Belarus. Although the team earned a dismal seventh place finish, Howden was second in scoring for the team, producing six points in six games. When the invitation to attend the Men's National Junior Team Summer Development Camp was sent out in the spring of 2010, Quinton's name was on the list.

Howden is a player making an impact, playing well for every Hockey Canada team he has been on and earning high praise from the coaching staff. In the 2010 NHL Entry Draft, Howden was selected in the 1st round, 25th overall by the Florida Panthers. Look for this young man on future Hockey Canada teams and in the pros.

SUMMER UPDATE

Howden played on Team White at the Men's National Junior Team Summer Development Camp in August. He didn't pick up any points but he contributed to his team winning both games.

In 2009–10 Howden was Moose Jaw's top scorer.

Howden played for Team West at the 2009 World Under-17 Hockey Challenge.

Season	Event	Team	GP	G	A	Pts	+/-	PIM	
REGULAR SEASON									
2009–10	WHL	Moose Jaw Warriors	65	28	37	65	14	44	
2008–09	WHL	Moose Jaw Warriors	62	13	17	30	-37	22	
2007–08	WHL	Moose Jaw Warriors	5	0	0	0	-4	0	
TOTALS			132	41	54	95	-27	66	
PLAYOFFS									
2010	WHL	Moose Jaw Warriors	2	0	2	2	-6	2	
TOTALS			2	0	2	2	-6	2	
HOCKEY CANADA									
Season	Event	Team	GP	G	A	PTS	+/-	PIM	
2010	IIHF World Under-18 Championship	Under 18	6	4	2	6	–	2	7th
2009	Memorial of Ivan Hlinka	Under 18	4	0	0	0	–	2	Gold
2009	WU17HC	West	6	3	1	4	–	10	4th

Boone Jenner

CANADA

Shoots: **Left**

Height: **6′1″**

Weight: **193 lbs**

Birthdate: **June 15, 1993**

Birthplace: **London, Ontario**

Hometown: **Dorchester, Ontario**

MHA: **Dorchester MHA**

Team: **Oshawa Generals, OHL**

NHL Draft: **2011 Eligibility**

Raised on a farm, seventeen-year-old Boone Jenner learned at an early age from his grandfather and father that honest, hard work was the key to success. When he got off the school bus at night, he put in his time haying, feeding cattle, fencing, repairing barns, and sometimes even shoveling manure. That work-hard philosophy combined with the fact that Boone also had two older brothers who constantly wrestled with him, knocking him flat on the kitchen floor, or played outdoor hockey with him has made him a tough, strong competitor. One of his brothers, 6′5″ Leo, played for the Plymouth Whalers and his other brother, Cole, played Junior B hockey in Ontario. Growing up the youngest, Boone learned that he had to keep up with his brothers. He is a hockey player who is willing to do the necessary things to improve his game. His work ethic is strong and he is willing to put in the time and sweat to get the job done.

Boone started playing hockey in Dorchester, a small town between Woodstock and London, Ontario, but after a few years it was evident that he was good enough to move on and play AAA. In his midget year, he played AAA minor midget for the Middlesex Elgin Chiefs as a centre, quickly becoming one of their best players and captain of the team. His toughness carried him through that year and he racked up a few penalty minutes although not many were for hooking or tripping. Most were checking penalties, teaching other players to steer clear, as they didn't want to take Jenner's punishment. He considered himself a

Boone is the youngest of three boys, all who played hockey.

Jenner captained Team Ontario in the 2010 World Under-17 Hockey Challenge.

Q&A

What is your favourite movie?
Dumb and Dumber

What is your favourite television show?
Two and a Half Men and *SportsCentre*

What is your favourite magazine?
The Hockey News

What is your pre-game meal?
Pasta with chicken

What is your favourite family meal?
Steak and potatoes

What are your favourite subjects in school?
Physical education and history

Who is your favourite band?
Nickelback

What is your favourite activity outside of hockey?
Golf

Who is your hockey hero?
Bobby Orr

Who are your heroes outside of hockey?
Terry Fox and my grandpa

What is your most memorable hockey experience?
My first goal in the OHL

What's something about yourself that most people don't know?
I grew up on a farm

What are your favourite things to do on long bus rides?
Watch movies and talk to my teammates

Who is your favourite superhero?
Superman

What is your favourite NHL team?
I like to see Canadian teams win

---

playmaker that year, and in the end he scored almost as many goals as assists. His tough play and his skill for getting points drew the attention of scouts.

In the 2009 OHL Priority Selection draft, Boone was drafted 4th overall by the Oshawa General's. After just one year with the Generals, Boone has made a name for himself as an outstanding all-around player, a fierce competitor, and a great faceoff player. Coach Chris DePiero used Boone in all situations, playing him a lot for a young guy, and consistently calling on him to take the big draws. Boone has a great wrist shot and is able to score by finding the offense. Not a razzle-dazzle player, Boone is steady, consistent, and always gives sixty minutes of good hockey. Although he is slotted as a power forward, he is still constantly working on improving the skating part of his game.

As a rookie with Oshawa, Boone played sixty-five games and earned nineteen goals and thirty assists. He finished fourth in scoring for the Generals and second among all OHL rookies, and he was named the Oshawa Generals Rookie of the Year. He was the OHL's Rookie of the Month for December. Then in April, he was named to the 2009–10 OHL First All-Rookie Team as their centre.

Backtrack a few months and Jenner was named the captain of Team Ontario at the 2010 World Under-17 Hockey Challenge. Boone led his team to the silver medal. The United States upset Team Ontario in the final game 2–1. Although Jenner is not the captain of his OHL team, he is still known to be a leader and good in the dressing room, a remarkable feat for a rookie, so look for him to wear a letter as he grows and matures. Jenner was invited to attend the Men's National Under-18 Team Summer Selection Camp in August 2010.

The Jenner boys are now all gone from the farm and Mr. Jenner has replaced his help with machines. When he hears that Boone is known for his work ethic it makes him proud.

Will Boone Jenner have what it takes to perhaps be on the Hockey Canada Under-18 team next spring and potentially a Hockey Canada World Junior player in future years? And does he have what it takes to excel in the pros? At this point Boone Jenner takes pride in his play, which is obvious to any onlooker. If he continues to follow the solid work-ethic advice of his family, he will be rewarded with a promising hockey future. Look for his name in the 2011 NHL Entry Draft.

SUMMER UPDATE

Jenner won gold at the Memorial of Ivan Hlinka with Canada's Summer U-18 team. In five games he tallied 2 goals and 1 assist to be 6th in overall scoring for the team.

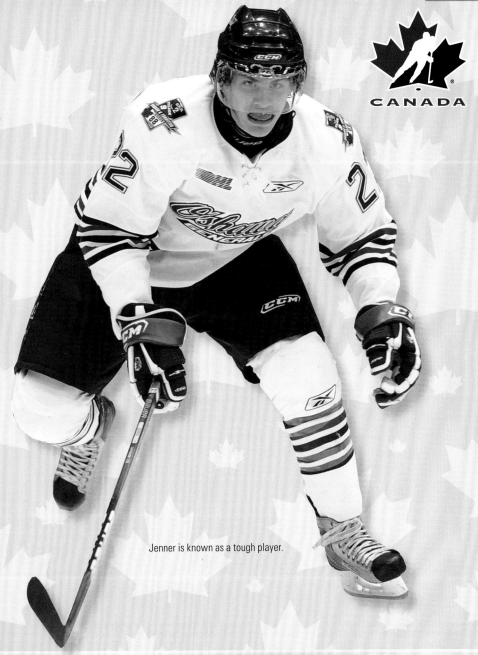

Jenner is known as a tough player.

Season	Event	Team	GP	G	A	Pts	+/-	PIM	
REGULAR SEASON									
2009–10	OHL	Oshawa Generals	65	19	30	49	-19	74	
TOTALS			65	19	30	49	-19	74	
HOCKEY CANADA									
Season	Event	Team	GP	G	A	PTS	+/-	PIM	
2010	WU17HC	Ontario	6	1	3	4	0/0	2	Silver

Ryan Johansen

Shoots: **Right**

Height: **6'3"**

Weight: **188 lbs**

Birthplace: **Vancouver, B.C.**

Hometown: **Port Moody, B.C.**

Birthdate: **July 31, 1992**

MHA: **Port Moody MHA**

Team: **Portland Winterhawks, WHL**

2010 NHL Entry Draft:
1st Round, 4th Overall, Columbus Blue Jackets

Often, late developers give up their dreams of being professional hockey players because they are regularly overlooked. But then there are those who ignore the disappointments and put up a fight, working hard on and off the ice, hoping that one day the combination of their skills and their future physical growth will enable them to play at an elite level. When he was finishing up his bantam draft year, Ryan Johansen was a scrawny kid that the majority of scouts passed over. Ultimately he was drafted in the 7th round, 150th overall, in the 2007 WHL bantam draft by the Portland Winterhawks, but it was clear, by the lack of correspondence, that they weren't all that interested in him.

So, Johansen decided his next best route would be to try for an NCAA scholarship. At the age of sixteen, he showed up at the Penticton Vees Junior A (the Vees play in the BCJHL) training camp and made the team. He started off on the Vees third and fourth lines but ended up playing on the second line and the power play. He carved out a modest seventeen points in forty-seven games. These numbers will not impress many, but he did continue to grow through the season, showing tremendous promise, and by the end of the season, he had definitely been noticed. During his year with Penticton, Ryan did indeed manage to get that NCAA Division 1 scholarship to Boston's Northeastern University.

But Ryan had to think twice about his scholarship after the newly hired general manager and head coach of the Portland

Ryan in 2008 at the NCAA Boston Tournament.

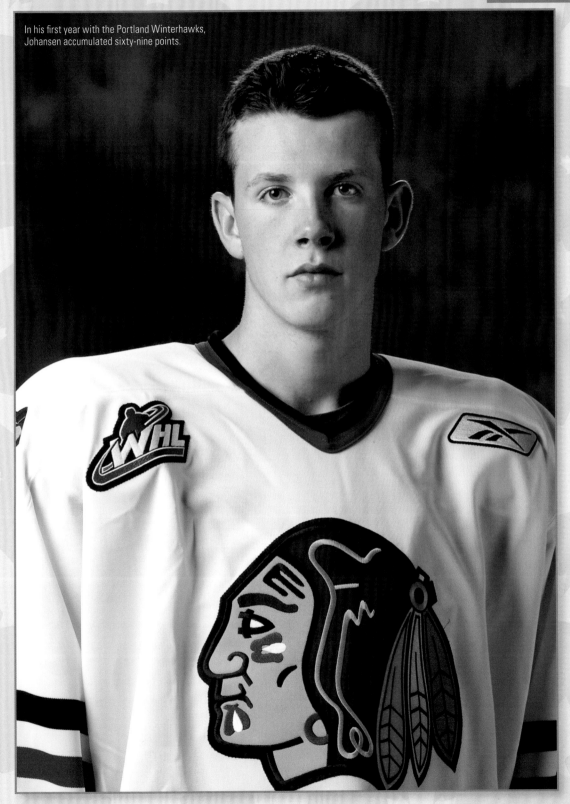

In his first year with the Portland Winterhawks, Johansen accumulated sixty-nine points.

Ryan Johansen

Q & A

What is your favourite movie?
The Hangover

What is your favourite
television show?
The Buried Life

What is your favourite book?
Playing with Fire

And your favourite magazine?
The Hockey News

What is your pre-game meal?
Carol's (mom) teriyaki
chicken

What is your favourite family
meal?
Chicken dinner

What is your favourite subject
in school?
Psychology

What is your favourite band?
Kings of Leon

What are your favourite activities
outside of hockey?
Golf and hanging out
with friends

Who are your hockey heroes?
Bobby Orr and
Joe Thornton

Who are your heroes outside
of hockey?
My parents

What is your most memorable
hockey experience?
Winning provincials
in my second year of
peewee hockey

What's something about yourself
that most people don't know?
I like to go bowling with
my friends

What is your favourite thing
to do on long bus rides?
Sleep

Who is your favourite superhero?
Batman

What is your favourite NHL team?
The San Jose Sharks and
Columbus Blue Jackets

Winterhawks, Mike Johnston, saw him playing that summer with some pro players in Langley, British Columbia. Johnston, who was a former assistant coach with the NHL's Los Angeles Kings and the Vancouver Canucks, definitely liked what he saw and made contact with Ryan.

At that point, and at the age of seventeen, Johansen had a big decision to make—he could pass up the scholarship and head to Portland—but was that the right move?

Turns out, it was. Johansen quickly excelled with the Winterhawks and within months was playing on one of their top lines. Johansen was definitely a contributing factor to the success of the Winterhawks in their 2009–10 season. For the first time in four years they made the playoffs, and they won a thrilling first round against the Spokane Chiefs with a game seven overtime victory. In their second round, the Winterhawks faced off against the talented Vancouver Giants and lost the series in a hard-fought six games. In his first WHL season, Johansen collected twenty-five goals and forty-four assists for a total of sixty-nine points, coming in second in scoring for the Winterhawks and second for all WHL rookies. In post-season play, Ryan earned nine points, and was the Winterhawks highest playoff scorer. Then when the 2010 NHL Entry Draft rolled around in June, Johansen went in the 1st round, 4th overall to the Columbus Blue Jackets.

Johansen has never played on any Hockey Canada teams.

Johansen is a gifted goal scorer.

CANADA

Ryan started playing hockey in Vancouver, but at the age of ten his family moved to Port Moody where Johansen played the rest of his minor hockey. Yes, he was smaller at the beginning of peewee hockey, but he never allowed his size to discourage him. He was a natural and gifted player whom his parents referred to as a "sportsaholic." Ryan's desire to play was intense from the beginning and he would plead with his parents to leave for his 6 a.m. Saturday morning practices extra early so he could get on the ice at 5:30 a.m. His sleepy parents would have to say, "Ryan, that is too early."

Johansen is one of the few players in this book who has yet to play for any Hockey Canada team. He didn't make the regional Under-17 team, nor was he selected for an Under-18 team. In the Hockey Canada system, players who mature early have a better chance of making those younger national teams. And Ryan Johansen is a late bloomer, still filling out and growing. But that is not to say he will never play for a Hockey Canada team. In fact, Johansen was invited to attend the Men's National Junior Team Summer Development Camp in August, 2010. Some players who grow later go on to become great hockey players, knowing rejection and, certainly, perseverance.

Johansen is a player who has kept his dreams alive, and has seen the results of determination. Fortunately for the hockey world, Ryan Johansen believes in himself.

SUMMER UPDATE

Johansen played for Team Red at the Men's National Junior Team Summer Development Camp in August. Red lost both games. He was one of three players on Team Red to earn 2 points (2 assists) in the two games.

Look for big things from Ryan Johansen.

The Next Ones

Ryan (*far right*) with fellow Winterhawk teammates (*from left to right*) Troy Rutkowski, Brad Ross, and Nino Niederreiter at the CHL/NHL Home Hardware Top Prospects Game.

Season	Event	Team	GP	G	A	Pts	+/-	PIM
		REGULAR SEASON						
2009–10	WHL	Portland Winterhawks	71	25	44	69	17	53
2008–09	WHL	Penticton Vees Jr. A	47	5	12	17	0	21
TOTALS			118	30	56	86	17	74
		PLAYOFFS						
2010	WHL	Portland Winterhawks	13	6	12	18	3	18
2009	BCJHL	Penticton Vees	10	4	3	7	0	2
TOTALS			23	10	15	25	3	20

Ryan Johansen

John McFarland

Shoots: **Right**

Height: **6'0"**

Weight: **197 lbs**

Birthdate: **April 2, 1992**

Birthplace: **Richmond Hill, Ontario**

Hometown: **Richmond Hill, Ontario**

Team: **Sudbury Wolves, OHL**

MHA: **Toronto Jr. Canadians MHA**

2010 NHL Entry Draft:
2nd Round, 33rd Overall, Florida Panthers

Even with a rotator cuff/AC shoulder injury inhibiting his play in his second year with the OHL Sudbury Wolves, John McFarland managed to get drafted early in the 2nd round, 33rd overall, by the Florida Panthers. And the previous year, his first year with Sudbury, McFarland was off with mononucleosis for 6 weeks. For the first few weeks with mono, McFarland didn't tell anyone that he was even feeling sick. Missing so many games two seasons in a row didn't hurt him as much as it could have. Obviously, the scouts saw something in this young man that rang bells, telling them to ignore his injuries and missed games, and focus on what he can do in the future.

McFarland is an extremely fast skater with good acceleration, and he loves to use his speed along the boards, often moving the puck by his opponents. Good balance on his skates keeps him upright and solid, plus he is strong on his stick and fairly strong overall, helping him to avoid getting crushed to the ice. With his strong skating skills, he is a forward who backchecks well and will drive back hard to step into a defensive role, making him a well-rounded player. In his second season with Sudbury, he was often used on the penalty kill, which definitely helped with developing some defensive play. McFarland is known as a player who plays with a lot of energy, and he has great intensity on the ice, always measuring himself against the best, wanting to be the best.

McFarland grew up in Richmond Hill, playing for the Vaughan Panthers at a very early age, and moving up to play for

McFarland went 1st overall in the 2008 OHL Priority Selection.

McFarland has great acceleration.

John McFarland

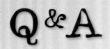

Q & A

What is your favourite movie?
Law Abiding Citizen

What is your favourite television channel?
TSN

What is your favourite book?
Tuesdays with Morrie

And your favourite magazine?
The Hockey News

What is your pre-game meal?
Chicken and rice

What is your favourite family meal?
Steak, potatoes, and salad

What is your favourite subject in school?
English

Who is your favourite band?
My Favorite Highway

What are your favourite activities outside of hockey?
Golf, fishing, working out, and hanging out with family and friends

Who is your hockey hero?
Jarome Iginla

Who is your hero outside of hockey?
Paul McFarland

What is your most memorable hockey experience?
Winning gold at Under-18 as captain of the team.

What's something about yourself that most people don't know?
I love to fish but don't like taking the fish off the hook

What is your favourite thing to do on long bus rides?
Hang out with teammates and watch movies

Who is your favourite superhero?
Spiderman

What is your favourite NHL team?
The Toronto Maple Leafs and the Florida Panthers

the Marlins, the Red Wings, and then finally the AAA Canadiens of the GTHL. In his last year with the Canadiens, in seventy-four games, McFarland scored one hundred goals and earned eighty-five assists. His 150 penalty minutes that year showed that he knows what it means to be a tough player.

When it came time for the 2008 OHL Priority Selection, John went 1st overall to the Sudbury Wolves, earning him the Jack Ferguson Award as the number one selection. Missing games for mono in his 2008–09 season, he still led the Sudbury rookies in scoring, place fourth in scoring for the Wolves, and ninth in OHL rookie scoring. That year he was also named Sudbury Rookie of the Year.

In January 2010, McFarland was selected to play for Team Orr the CHL/NHL Home Hardware Top Prospects Game and he also competed in the Home Hardware Skills Competition, scoring three goals in the three-on-three game.

Like most young hockey players in Canada, one of McFarland's goals is to play on the Hockey Canada World Junior Team. So far, his experience on Hockey Canada's teams is solid. In April of 2010, he was named captain for the Canadian Under-18 team. He competed in the IIHF World Under-18 Championship in Belarus, and although the team finished seventh, McFarland put in a good performance, securing five points in six games. Just prior to that tournament, in 2009, at the Christmas tryout camp for the 2010 IIHF World Junior Team, John was cut, but the fact that he was invited at only seventeen was still a huge accomplishment. This invite came because he was one of three younger years to play on the Under-18 team in 2009, finishing fourth at the IIHF World Under-18 Championship in Fargo, North Dakota. Plus, McFarland was also a member of the 2009 Memorial of Ivan Hlinka team that won gold, finishing as the third top scorer for Canada with four goals and three assists in four games. Months prior to those tournaments, in January 2009, McFarland won a gold medal with Team Ontario at the 2009 World Under-17 Hockey Challenge and was named to the tournament All-Star Team. It is safe to say Hockey Canada will be looking at his play in the fall to determine whether he secures a spot on the upcoming team.

This is a young player with a lot of heart and determination, coupled with great speed, a good shot, and a strong vision on the ice. So far none of his injuries or illnesses have deterred him from taking that next step to the pros. He is looking forward to a healthy year with Sudbury, a profession in the pros, and perhaps a shot at a future Hockey Canada team.

SUMMER UPDATE

McFarland did not attend the Men's National Junior Team Summer Development Camp in August but will definitely be looked at by the scouts this fall as he plays for the Sudbury Wolves.

McFarland playing a tough game of hockey.

Season	Event	Team	GP	G	A	Pts	+/-	PIM	
			REGULAR SEASON						
2009–10	OHL	Sudbury Wolves	64	20	30	50	-17	70	
2008–09	OHL	Sudbury Wolves	58	21	31	52	-30	36	
TOTALS			122	41	61	102	-47	106	
			PLAYOFFS						
2010	OHL	Sudbury Wolves	4	3	0	3	-1	2	
2009	OHL	Sudbury Wolves	6	1	3	4	-1	2	
TOTALS			10	4	3	7	-2	4	

			HOCKEY CANADA						
Season	Event		Team	GP	G	A	PTS	+/-	PIM	
2010	IIHF World Under-18 Championship		Under 18	6	4	1	5	–	8	7th
2009	Memorial of Ivan Hlinka		Under 18	4	4	3	7	–	6	Gold
2009	IIHF World Under-18 Championship		Under 18	6	3	5	8	–	6	4th
2009	WU17HC		Ontario	6	9	4	13	–	4	Gold

John McFarland

Ryan Nugent-Hopkins

Shoots: **Left**

Height: **6'0"**

Weight: **160 lbs**

Birthdate: **April 12, 1993**

Birthplace: **Burnaby, British Columbia**

Hometown: **Burnaby, British Columbia**

Team: **Red Deer Rebels, WHL**

MHA: **Burnaby MHA**

NHL Draft: **2011 Eligibility**

After winning the British Columbia AAA scoring race when he was playing in the British Columbia Major Midget League with the Vancouver Giants, and winning the scoring title at the Mac's Midget tournament in Calgary, Alberta at Christmas, it is no surprise that the WHL has embraced Ryan Nugent-Hopkins. His Red Deer Rebel coach is very vocal about this up-and-coming young player and more than willing to talk about how special he is as a player and a person.

Even with all his accolades, Ryan is a humble individual who faces every challenge head-on and does so in an unassuming way. This kid sees the ice well and thinks the game through. With his good puck-handling skills and his remarkable agility and ability to hang onto the puck in traffic, rolling off checks and slithering his way toward the net, he will be someone the scouts watch carefully next year when it is time for the NHL draft.

Nugent-Hopkins played minor hockey with the North Shore Winter Club and then the Burnaby Winter Club. Yes, he tried some other sports like baseball and track and field, and although he was good in track and looked into pursuing it at the club level, it just didn't work because it always conflicted with hockey.

Nugent-Hopkins is a Burnaby boy and wanted to play hockey from the time he could walk.

Nugent-Hopkins went 1st overall in the 2008
WHL bantam draft to the Red Deer Rebels.

Ryan Nugent-Hopkins

Q & A

What is your favourite movie?
Seabiscuit

What are your favourite television shows?
The Simpsons and *Friends*

What is your favourite book?
Life of Pi

And your favourite magazine?
Sports Illustrated

What is your pre-game meal?
Penne alfredo and chicken

What is your favourite family meal?
BBQ steak

What is your favourite subject in school?
Construction

Who is your favourite band?
The Fray

What are your favourite activities outside of hockey?
Playing pool and NHL 2010 on Xbox

Who is your hockey hero?
Maurice Richard

Who are your heroes outside of hockey?
My parents and my brother

What is your most memorable hockey experience?
Playing in the Macs Midget Final

Tell us something about yourself that most people don't know?
I have two middle names, Jarromie and Noel

What is your favourite thing to do on long bus rides?
Sleep

Who is your favourite superhero?
Batman

What is your favourite NHL team?
The Ottawa Senators and the Pittsburgh Penguins

None of his success in hockey was driven by his parents, in fact his mother is quite overwhelmed by her son's success. When he was just five, his parents divorced and Ryan handled it all extremely well, taking everything in stride. His parents kept their business away from the children, working amicably with shared custody. As a result, Ryan remained well-adjusted and was a team player at home. And he also became a solid team player on the ice, a character trait he has continued to hone and perfect.

The success in his early years saw him move up levels and he was soon playing with older kids but none of that fazed Ryan. He learned to focus to achieve even greater success, and in the process remain humble. In the 2008 WHL bantam draft the Red Deer Rebels, who had 1st selection, wasted no time in announcing that their pick was Ryan Nugent-Hopkins of Burnaby, British Columbia. They felt he stood in a class of his own.

In the fall of 2009, Ryan headed from Vancouver to Red Deer where he became a force on the ice and a popular kid in the dressing room. With no negative attitude, he is all about the team. He played on the top two lines all year and did exceptionally well for a rookie. He may not be the biggest player on the bench, but what he lacks in size, he makes up for with intelligence. He has an unbelievable backhand shot, a good forehand shot, and is a fantastic skater with great edge control. What is most effective in his skating, however, is his quick acceleration which just seems to come naturally to him. At the end of Red Deer's season, (they lost to the Saskatoon Blades in the first round of the playoffs), Ryan was awarded the Rookie of the Year award. His awards didn't end with just his own team. Nugent-Hopkins was also awarded the Jim Piggott Memorial Trophy and the WHL Eastern Conference Rookie of the Year. He also was a runner-up for the CHL Rookie of the Year award.

This young lad has also been on a Hockey Canada Roster. He was selected to play for Team Pacific at the 2010 World Under-17 Hockey Challenge in Timmins, Ontario, finishing fifth. And more recently, he attended the Men's National Under-18 Team Summer Selection Camp.

With his confidence, humility, and top-end skill set, Ryan Nugent-Hopkins is a name that will keep popping up in the hockey world. In the fall of 2010, it is more than likely that his name will be mentioned as one of the top WHL draft picks as he heads into his draft year. Hockey Canada is also looking at him for future teams. All this young lad has to do is more of the same: maintain his focus and drive. And, of course, if he keeps his humility and great attitude in the process, he will become a much better hockey player and person. Look for him in the 2011 NHL Entry Draft.

Nugent-Hopkins ready to score for Team Pacific in the 2010 World Under-17 Hockey Challenge.

SUMMER UPDATE

Nugent-Hopkins had a fantastic U-18 tournament at the Memorial of Ivan Hlinka. He was tied for Canada's top scorer with 5 goals and 2 assists for 7 points. Nugent-Hopkins also scored the lone goal in the final game where Canada beat the USA 1–0 to take the gold.

CANADA

Season	Event	Team	GP	G	A	Pts	+/-	PIM	
REGULAR SEASON									
2009–10	WHL	Red Deer Rebels	67	24	41	65	-4	28	
2008–09	WHL	Red Deer Rebels	5	2	4	6	-6	0	
TOTALS			72	26	45	71	-10	28	
PLAYOFFS									
2010	WHL	Red Deer Rebels	4	0	2	2	-2	0	
TOTALS			4	0	2	2	-2	0	
HOCKEY CANADA									
Season	Event	Team	GP	G	A	PTS	+/-	PIM	
2010	WU17HC	Pacific	5	1	4	5	–	6	5th

Matt Puempel

Shoots: **Left**

Height: **6'0"**

Weight: **190 lbs**

Birthdate: **January 24, 1993**

Birthplace: **Windsor, Ontario**

Hometown: **Essex, Ontario**

Team: **Peterborough Petes, OHL**

MHA: **Essex MHA**

NHL Draft: **2011 Eligibility**

For the months of January, February, and March of 2010, Peterborough Petes' Matt Puempel was named the OHL Rookie of the Month. In March alone he scored sixteen points (seven goals and nine assists) helping the Petes win their final four games in their regular season to take sixth place in the eastern conference standings. In four of those five games he scored more than one point, and in the last game on March 13, he managed to rack up the points by scoring a hat trick—his second of the season—as well as three assists to make it a six-point total which also earned him the first star of the game. For the week ending March 14, he was named the Boston Pizza OHL and CHL Player of the Week. Then the big awards started coming his way. Puempel was named OHL Rookie of the Year in April 2010, and he picked up four awards at the Petes annual awards banquet: Best Combining Scholastics and Hockey; having the most 3-Star nominations; Rookie of the Year; and MVP as voted by his teammates. Puempel finished off his award-winning rookie year by winning the CHL Rookie of the Year award. Not bad for a kid who was only sixteen when he started with the Petes.

As a young first-year player with the Petes, Matt was a strong character player whose maturity allowed him to immediately fit in with the team. He was well liked and always did the right things. The Petes drafted him 6th overall in the 2009 OHL Priority Selection and, with his growth spurt in the second half

Matt played minor hockey in Essex until he started into AAA hockey.

The Next Ones

Puempel racked up sixty-four points for the Petes in his first year in the OHL.

of the season, they were not disappointed in their choice. Puempel finished off his year with thirty-three goals and thirty-one assists for sixty-four points in fifty-nine games to lead all OHL Rookies.

Puempel played his early hockey in Essex but it wasn't long before he was noticed by the AAA coaches and started playing in Windsor Sun County, mostly with players who were a year older. When he was young he also liked to play in net but because he was such a gifted forward he didn't pursue goaltending. To fill his desire to play in net, Matt donned the heavy, large pads and put himself in front of the lacrosse ball. He was darn good at catching and blocking, playing at a high level in the sport. But the time came when he had to choose between lacrosse and hockey.

Hockey Canada was thankful for this decision Matt made as he was selected to play for Team Ontario at the 2010 World Under-17 Hockey Challenge, helping his team with five points (two goals and three assists) in six games to capture the silver medal, losing to the United States in a 2–1 battle. Puempel was also invited to attend the Men's National Under-18 Team Summer Selection Camp in August 2010.

With a great shot and a knack for the net, Matt has a good future in front of him as a professional and Hockey Canada player. His skill for hanging around the net is becoming more and more refined every time he steps on the ice, and it is obvious that he is learning the offensive zone well. Coupled with his offensive net talent, he is also a player who is willing to go to the dirty areas to score goals.

Although he did score his fair share of goals this year, he also worked on specific areas that will help him become a total forward package. He definitely improved his defensive play, working constantly on the little things to become that solid two-way player scouts and coaches are looking for. As with any young player, his coaches have talked to him about what he needs to work on and, yes, he is a good skater, but this is something he will continue to work on. Strength on his skates will come with age, physical maturity, and hard work off the ice.

None of the hard work frightens Puempel because he is a regimented athlete who is conscious about his nutrition and works with a personal trainer.

Combine an honest gift for scoring goals and a strong work ethic and you have a player who is destined for great things in the hockey world. Over the few short years that Matt Puempel has been playing hockey, his skills have been noticed and he has made some great strides. What is in his future? That will be determined in the next few years, but two things are for sure: the Peterborough Petes will welcome him back next fall and Hockey Canada will be looking at him for future teams.

CANADA

Puempel played very strong with Canada's Summer U-18 Team in the Memorial of Ivan Hlinka tournament. He was tied for top scorer with Nugent-Hopkins with 3 goals and 4 assists for a total of 7 points.

Puempel dodging a stick as he races for the puck in the 2010 World Under-17 Hockey Challenge.

Season	Event	Team	GP	G	A	Pts	+/-	PIM	
REGULAR SEASON									
2009–10	OHL	Peterborough Petes	59	33	31	64	-2	43	
TOTALS			59	33	31	64	-2	43	
PLAYOFFS									
2010	OHL	Peterborough Petes	4	1	1	2	0	6	
TOTALS			4	1	1	2	0	6	
HOCKEY CANADA									
Season	Event	Team	GP	G	A	PTS	+/-	PIM	
2010	WU17HC	Ontario	6	2	3	5	–	0	Silver

Matt Puempel

Brad Ross

CANADA

Shoots: **Left**

Height: **6'1"**

Weight: **173 lbs**

Birthdate: **May 28, 1992**

Birthplace: **Edmonton, Alberta**

Hometown: **Lethbridge, Alberta**

Team: **Portland Winterhawks, WHL**

MHA: **Lethbridge MHA**

2010 NHL Entry Draft:
2nd Round, 43rd Overall, Toronto Maple Leafs

A fun-loving, happy-go-lucky, big-hearted kid off the ice, WHL Portland Winterhawks player Brad Ross is anything but that when he straps on his skates and sets foot on the ice. This young man is known as an agitator, and to be a gritty, hard-working, and even downright nasty opponent at times. Not afraid to go to the corners, he definitely gets things done by playing physical, Canadian-style hockey. He finishes his checks—and he does check a lot—and he is a player who definitely keeps the opposition off balance. He fights when he has to, and stirs it up when called upon. He loves to chirp and is extremely competitive. When the game is over, he takes off the skates and becomes the nice guy and social leader of the Portland Winterhawks.

Brad started his minor hockey in Cochrane, Alberta, playing his first year with the Cremona Cougars and then the following few years with Cochrane Minor Hockey Association. Ross' father is an RCMP officer, and when he was transferred to Lethbridge in 2002, Brad started playing with the Lethbridge Minor Hockey Association, mostly on AAA teams. In his Bantam AAA year, (2006–07), Ross was thrilled to be coached by Rich Sutter. Brad was part of a strong team that went the distance only to face a devastating loss in the provincial finals in an overtime game. When the season ended, Ross found himself at the high end of the WHL bantam draft, going in the 1st round, 5th overall to the Moose Jaw Warriors who then immediately traded him to the

Brad began playing minor hockey in Cochrane, Alberta before moving to Lethbridge.

On the ice, Ross is a tough competitor.

What is your favourite movie?
How the Grinch Stole Christmas

What is your favourite
television show?
Family Guy

What is your favourite book?
Holes

And your favourite magazine?
The Hockey News

What is your pre-game meal?
Pasta

What is your favourite
family meal?
Pizza

What is your favourite subject
in school?
Physical education

What is your favourite band?
Def Leppard

What are your favourite activities
outside of hockey?
Golfing and hanging out
with friends

Who is your hockey hero?
Saku Koivu

Who is your hero outside
of hockey?
Jim Carrey

What is your most memorable
hockey experience?
Getting drafted to the
Maple Leafs

What's something about yourself
that most people don't know?
I'm really not a
morning person

What is your favourite thing
to do on long bus rides?
Listen to music

Who is your favourite superhero?
Spiderman

What is your favourite NHL team?
The Toronto Maple Leafs

Portland Winterhawks. He played midget hockey in Lethbridge, but Portland did pull him up to play for three games at the end of the season when he was fifteen.

Moving into the WHL at sixteen, 2008–09, was a good move for Ross since he had the tenacity and ability to handle the big boys. He never shied away from anyone, no matter the size, showing his true grit from the onset. At the end of the season, he had 119 penalty minutes and was named Portland's Rookie of the Year. His scoring sat at nine goals and seventeen assists for twenty-six points.

Then in the 2009–10 season, Ross, one year older and wiser, and knowing it was his NHL Draft year, decided to change his offensive stats. At the end of the season, in seventy-one games, he scored twenty-seven goals and helped his teammates with forty-one assists to record a total of sixty-eight points. In raising his stats he also upped his penalty minutes to a whopping 203.

Reports prior to the NHL Draft talked about Brad and how perhaps he wasn't quite big enough to play his style of game in the NHL. But not everyone saw him this way. His production in his 2009–10 season coupled with his penalty minutes was enough to help his Draft position. He went in the 2nd round, 43rd overall to the Toronto Maple Leafs. Hockey guru and General Manager of the Toronto Maple Leafs, Brian Burke, chose Ross as the Leafs number one pick. Prior to the Draft, Brad had attended the NHL Combine, producing great interviews and was found to be a confident, interesting, take-charge young man.

Ross has also been a steady component in the Hockey Canada system. In 2009, he played for Team Pacific at the World Under-17 Hockey Challenge in Port Alberni winning a silver medal. Then he also played in the 2009 Memorial of Ivan Hlinka Under-18, taking home a gold medal at that tournament.

On the hockey bus with his teammates Ross is always surrounded by six guys. They laugh and talk and have a good time. On the ice Ross also gets in the scrum. Off the ice he wants to have fun and on the ice he wants to be an agitator. In both situations he is emotionally involved. At present, Ross definitely has enough skills to be a playmaker; he showed that with Portland, but like any young player he must continue to improve. With continual honing, practice, and dedication this young man has all the potential to emerge as a threat on a Hockey Canada National Junior Team and to be a good player in the NHL.

SUMMER UPDATE
Unfortunately Ross was sidelined at the Men's National Junior Team Summer Development Camp in August with a groin injury.

Ross likes to play physical, Canadian hockey.

Season	Event	Team	GP	G	A	Pts	+/-	PIM	
REGULAR SEASON									
2009–10	WHL	Portland Winterhawks	71	27	41	68	22	203	
2008–09	WHL	Portland Winterhawks	61	9	17	26	-16	119	
2007–08	WHL	Portland Winterhawks	3	0	0	0	0	0	
TOTALS			135	36	58	94	6	322	
PLAYOFFS									
2010	WHL	Portland Winterhawks	13	2	7	9	-2	36	
TOTALS			13	2	7	9	-2	36	
HOCKEY CANADA									
Season	Event	Team	GP	G	A	PTS	+/-	PIM	
2009	Memorial of Ivan Hlinka	Under 18	4	0	1	1	–	0	Gold
2009	WU17HC	Pacific	6	1	2	3	–	10	Silver

Jaden Schwartz

CANADA

Shoots: **Left**

Height: **5'9.5"**

Weight: **172 lbs**

Birthdate: **June 25, 1992**

Birthplace: **Melfort, Saskatchewan**

Hometown: **Wilcox, Saskatchewan**

Team: **Tri-City Storm, USHL**

MHA: **Melfort MHA**

2010 NHL Entry Draft:
1st Round, 14th Overall, St. Louis Blues

Taking a different route to the pros, Jaden Schwartz opted out of playing in the Canadian Hockey League and instead played with the Tri-City Storm of the USHL (United States Hockey League), which has given him a scholarship to attend Colorado College in the fall of 2010. His route didn't hurt his chances when the 2010 NHL Entry Draft rolled around in June. Schwartz was picked up in the 1st round, 14th overall by the St. Louis Blues.

His time in the USHL served Jaden well as he was named the CCM USHL Forward of the Year for the 2009–10 season, which is an award that the league coaches vote on. There is good reason why Schwartz was voted as the best forward. He won the USHL scoring title with thirty-three goals and fifty assists for a total of eighty-three points, breaking the record for the most points scored in this league since the 2001–02 season. He is the youngest player to lead the USHL in scoring since the 1982–83 season.

So what prompted this young man to deviate from the typical path of young hockey players in Canada? He was drafted by Tri-City in the 2007 WHL bantam draft as their 8th round selection, 173rd overall. After being selected, when he was just fourteen-years-old, the Schwartz family went on a holiday. They travelled through Washington and Colorado to visit where the WHL Tri-City Americans played, where the USHL Tri-City Storm played, and to visit Colorado College.

Schwartz is a true Saskatchewan boy.

Schwartz has played for Hockey Canada in U-18, U-17, and also for Canada West in the World Junior A Challenge.

Q&A

What are your favourite movies?

Happy Gilmore and
Remember the Titans

What is your favourite
television show?

SportsCentre and *The Office*

What is your favourite book?

The Tunnels

And your favourite magazine?

The Hockey News

What is your pre-game meal?

Eggs

What is your favourite
family meal?

Steak and
homemade burgers

What is your favourite subject
in school?

History

Who is your favourite singer?

Carrie Underwood

What is your favourite activity
outside of hockey?

Football

Who are your hockey heroes?

Joe Sakic and
Sidney Crosby

Who is your hero outside
of hockey?

My sister, Mandi

What is your most memorable
hockey experience?

Winning gold at the Ivan
Hlinka tournament in 2009

What's something about yourself
that most people don't know?

I used to be a quarterback,
and won the high school
championship with
Notre Dame

What is your favourite thing to do
on long bus rides?

Sleep and talk with guys
on the team

Who is your favourite superhero?

Batman

What is your favourite NHL team?

The Colorado Avalanche,
the Pittsburgh Penguins
and the St. Louis Blues

Jaden was leaning toward the idea of going to college, but knew his final decision would be a tough one.

Jaden, along with his parents and siblings returned home to Wilcox, Saskatchewan, with the understanding that they had one more year for Jaden to make his decision. All three of the Schwartz children attended Notre Dame and Jaden's parents had moved to Wilcox, Saskatchewan, knowing they could commute back and forth to Regina, so none of the kids would have to billet.

That next year, 2007–08, Jaden played midget AAA hockey for Notre Dame and ramped up his offensive skills by leading the Saskatchewan Midget AAA Hockey League in scoring and being named the SMAAHL top forward. He also played in the Mac's Midget tournament that Christmas (2008), a tournament he had played in the previous year, winning gold.

The following year, when Jaden could have made his debut with Tri-City in the WHL, he made the decision to stay at home with his family, playing on the Notre Dame Saskatchewan Junior Hockey League (SJHL) team at sixteen. Many players leave home at sixteen, but Jaden decided to stay at home for one more year. Once again he made a name for himself with his offensive talents by coming in second in scoring and fifth in the SJHL scoring. He also led all SJHL rookies in scoring and was named SJHL Rookie of the Year and named to the All-Rookie Team.

When he was seventeen, Jaden decided he wanted to pursue a college scholarship so he left home to play with the Tri-City Storm. With his high scoring, Schwartz helped take this team to the playoffs in the 2009–10 season, so he was unable to participate in the IIHF World Under-18 Championships. In the spring of 2010,

Jaden playing outside in Saskatchewan.

The Next Ones

Schwartz with the Notre Dame Hounds.

CANADA

Schwartz was invited to the Men's National Junior Team Summer Development Camp.

He has served some time, however, with Hockey Canada, having played for Team West at the 2009 World Under-17 Hockey Challenge, finishing 4th, and winning a silver medal at the 2008 World Junior A Hockey Challenge in Camrose, Alberta. Jaden was also a member of the Memorial of Ivan Hlinka Under-18, gold-winning team in 2009.

Jaden is one of those players who can push his own game up a notch, and when he's on the ice he has the ability to make his teammates do the same. Fans love to watch him play as he is dynamic around the net, which is obvious from his impressive scoring records.

A goal-scorer with a great head on his shoulders, Jaden's strength comes from his family and their strong values. His older sister, Mandi, earned an NCAA Division-One Scholarship at Yale University, but has been in and out of the hospital after she was diagnosed with leukemia. In remission, she went back to Yale in January 2010, but in the spring the leukemia returned and the Schwartz family desperately searched for a bone-marrow match. Jaden went to the 2010 NHL Entry Draft knowing how desperate his sister was for a bone-marrow match and did what he could in every interview to spread the news. They have been through a lot, but Jaden stays grounded and positive. He names his sister as his hero. He will no doubt have a great season with Colorado College in the 2010–11 season.

SUMMER UPDATE

While at the Men's National Junior Team Summer Development Camp, Schwartz found out his sister Mandi had found a match for a stem cell transplant. The transplant was set for August 26th. With this news, Schwartz had a great second game. Playing for Team White he scored 1 goal and earned 1 assist for a total of 2 points.

Schwartz is a dynamic player around the net.

Schwartz is a fan pleaser.

Duncan

Season	Event	Team	GP	G	A	Pts	+/-	PIM	
REGULAR SEASON									
2009–10	USHL	Tri-City Storm	60	33	50	83	-6	18	
2008–09	SJHL	Notre Dame Jr. A Hounds	46	34	42	76	0	15	
HOCKEY CANADA									
Season	Event	Team	GP	G	A	PTS	+/-	PIM	
2009	Memorial of Ivan Hlinka	Under 18	4	2	2	4	–	0	Gold
2009	WU17HC	West	6	2	4	6	–	2	4th
2008	WJAC	CAN-W	4	0	4	4	–	0	Silver

Tyler Seguin

Shoots: **Right**

Height: **6'1"**

Weight: **179 lbs**

Birthdate: **January 31, 1992**

Birthplace: **Brampton, Ontario**

Hometown: **Brampton, Ontario**

Team: **Plymouth Whalers, OHL**

MHA: **Toronto Young Nationals MHA**

2010 NHL Entry Draft:
1st Round, 2nd Overall, Boston Bruins

Tyler Seguin and Taylor Hall were the two most popular players for the entire 2009–10 hockey season in anticipation of who would be selected first in the 2010 NHL Entry Draft. There is always such speculation, wonderment, and excitement to see who will enter the history books, being named the the number one draft pick each season. Every hockey expert will have their own opinions and reasons. In the 2010 NHL Entry Draft all eyes were on both of these young men, and in the end it was Taylor number one, with Seguin right behind him in the 1st round, 2nd overall by the Boston Bruins.

The chances of fans seeing Tyler Seguin play in the World Junior Team at Christmas are a bit watered down and for good reason. If he sees any success during his debut 2010–11 season in the NHL with the Bruins, his team is unlikely to free him to don the red and white jersey for Canada at the 2011 IIHF World Junior Championship in Buffalo, New York. In the spring of 2010, he was definitely on the invite list for the Men's National Junior Team Summer Development Camp, taking place in August.

Seguin has spent some time with Hockey Canada teams but in December of 2009 he suffered a big blow when he was cut from the 2010 team. It is rare for a seventeen-year-old to make the National Junior Team, but Seguin had been having such a great season that he was disappointed in the final outcome. He has, however, won a gold medal with Team Ontario at the 2009

Tyler showing off one of many, many trophies that he has won over his minor hockey years.

Seguin has always been an All-Star.

Q & A

What is your favourite movie?
Never Back Down

What is your favourite
television show?
NHL on the Fly

What is your favourite book?
The Alchemist

And your favourite magazine?
The Hockey News

What is your pre-game meal?
Rice and chicken

What is your favourite
family meal?
Steak and potatoes

What is your favourite subject
in school?
Public speaking

What is your favourite band?
Theory of a Deadman

What are your favourite activities
outside of hockey?
Golf and fishing

Who is your hockey hero?
Steve Yzerman

Who is your hero outside
of hockey?
My dad

What is your most memorable
hockey experience?
Winning the Under-18
gold medal

What's something about yourself
that most people don't know?
I love going to the movies

What is your favourite thing
to do on long bus rides?
Listen to my iPod

Who is your favourite superhero?
Superman

What is your favourite NHL team?
The Boston Bruins

World Under-17 Hockey Challenge and he also won a gold medal with the Under-18 team at the Memorial of the Ivan Hlinka in the Czech Republic in August 2009. He would have played for the Under-18 team in the spring of 2010, but the Plymouth Whalers managed to get to the semifinals of the OHL Western Conference playoffs, getting beat by Taylor Hall's team, the Windsor Spitfires.

It takes courage and determination to overcome a disappointment and move on.

Seguin did just that, playing hard and strong enough that even up to the last minute before the NHL Entry Draft, he was still ranked by many as the potential 1st draft pick.

There is good reason why his name was still selected as number one by some. Seguin did take home a bit of hardware at the end of the 2009–10 season, winning the OHL's most prestigious Red Tilson Trophy as OHL's Most Outstanding Player of the Year, which is an award voted by the writers and broadcasters that cover the league. He also won the Jack Link's Top Prospect of the Year award at the CHL awards banquet. Seguin finished his regular season with 106 points, (48 goals and 58 assists), and tied for first overall in total points in the OHL.

Seguin was Plymouth's 1st round selection, 9th overall, in the 2008 OHL Priority Selection. In his first year with Plymouth he ended up third in scoring and he led all Plymouth rookies in goals, assists, and points. He was also third in OHL rookie scoring, was the highest scoring Canadian in the OHL, fourth in OHL rookie playoff scoring, runner-up for the OHL Rookie of the Year award, named Plymouth Rookie of the Year, and named to the OHL first All-Rookie Team. And this was all in a season where he didn't score his first goal until fifteen games into the season. In his second year with Plymouth, he saw a lot more ice time, and that's when he really started racking up the points. At the CHL/NHL Home Hardware Top Prospects Game in January 2010, Seguin was named captain of Team Orr.

Seguin is an outstanding skater, having three speeds, and he uses all of them all the time. Naturally talented as a playmaker, he has the uncanny ability to make everyone around him better. Coaches love this kind of player. Off the ice he is a hard worker in the weight room and is constantly trying to improve his game. From year one to year two in the OHL, Seguin worked on his scoring and from just a quick glance at his stats it is obvious that the work paid off. Like every young, gifted goal-scorer, Seguin has to work on his defensive play, especially down low.

Seguin played most of his minor hockey with Brampton and in the GTHL. His father had a hockey scholarship to the University of Vermont and Tyler toyed with pursuing that route but in the end he chose to play for the Plymouth Whalers because they offered him something no other team could: a strong education package.

Tyler winning the Top Draft Prospect Award at the CHL Awards Banquet in 2010.

TOP DRAFT PROSPECT
MEILLEUR ESPOIR PROFESSIONNEL

So Seguin packed his bags and moved from the all-boys school he attended in Toronto to attend a co-ed American high school with three times the student population. He adjusted to the school of six thousand kids, his good natured personality allowing him to fit in right away.

Seguin has his emotions figured out and understands when to be serious in the dressing room and when it's time to loosen up. He has a reputation for being the funny one. Perhaps it is this easy-going personality that has allowed him to sit back, watch, wait, and then move in for the attack when needed. This is a young player who has dealt with a few disappointments already so his skin is thick and he's ready to take on the world of professional hockey. Many are predicting that he will be the "Next One" to have a long career in the pros.

SUMMER UPDATE

Seguin played for Team Red and scored a lone goal. It was his first game since the spring.

Seguin is a terrific skater and uses all speeds effectively.

The Next Ones

Seguin won his first Hockey Canada gold medal when Team Ontario won the World Under-17 Hockey Challenge in 2009.

Season	Event	Team	GP	G	A	Pts	+/-	PIM	
		REGULAR SEASON							
2009–10	OHL	Plymouth Whalers	63	48	58	106	17	54	
2008–09	OHL	Plymouth Whalers	61	21	46	67	14	28	
TOTALS			124	69	104	173	31	82	
		PLAYOFFS							
2010	OHL	Plymouth Whalers	9	5	5	10	-5	8	
2009	OHL	Plymouth Whalers	11	5	11	16	1	8	
TOTALS			20	10	16	26	-4	16	
		HOCKEY CANADA							
Season	Event	Team	GP	G	A	PTS	+/-	PIM	
2009	Memorial of Ivan Hlinka	Under 18	4	4	6	10	–	6	Gold
2009	WU17HC	Ontario	6	3	8	11	–	8	Gold

Riley Sheahan

CANADA

Shoots: **Left**

Height: **6'2"**

Weight: **200 lbs**

Birthdate: **December 7, 1991**

Birthplace: **St. Catharines, Ontario**

Hometown: **St. Catharines, Ontario**

Team: **University of Notre Dame Fighting Irish, CCHA**

MHA: **St. Catharines MHA**

2010 NHL Entry Draft:
1st Round, 21st Overall, Detroit Red Wings

Here's a young man who has yet to play on a Hockey Canada team, though through stubborn determination, hard work, and a love of the game, he was recently invited to attend the Men's National Junior Team Summer Development Camp in the summer of 2010. In 2008, Riley Sheahan didn't quite make the cut for Team Ontario to play in the World Under-17 Hockey Challenge, nor did he ever make any Under-18 team in Canada. But none of those disappointments have stopped Sheahan from trying to fulfill his dream to play for Canada's World Junior team and to be a NHL player.

Sheahan has just kept working at improving his skills, and now everything is staring to click for this young man. Along with the prestigious invite to the National Junior Camp, Sheahan went in the 1st round, 21st overall in the 2010 NHL Entry Draft,to the prestigious Detroit Red Wings. Red Wings General Manager, Ken Holland saw real potential in Sheahan and took him as their 1st round pick.

Most players follow the CHL route to get to the top of the heap but Riley made a decision in his early teens to go to college even though he knew this path could negatively impact his chances to make a Hockey Canada team or see the NHL Entry Draft. College hockey schedules see far fewer games than CHL hockey, so it is difficult for scouts to get a good look at players, and as a result they don't always land on the radar. In the 2007 OHL Priority Selection draft, Sheahan was picked by the Erie

Sheahan played minor hockey in St. Catharines, Ontario.

Riley with his sister Karli at the 2010 NHL Entry Draft.

Q & A

What is your favourite movie?
Get him to the Greek

What is your favourite television show?
Rob Dyrdeck's Fantasy Factory

What is your favourite book?
The Kite Runner

And your favourite magazine?
The Hockey News

What is your pre-game meal?
Pasta, chicken, and salad

What is your favourite family meal?
Pizza and wings

What is your favourite subject in school?
Physical education

Who are your favourite musicians?
Kenny Chesney, John Mayer, and Amos Lee

What are your favourite activities outside of hockey?
Playing guitar, mountain biking, and basketball

Who is your hockey hero?
Rick Nash

Who are your heroes outside of hockey?
My parents

What is your most memorable hockey experience?
Playing in the High School Hockey OFSAA Championship

What's something about yourself that most people don't know?
I used to enjoy basketball more than hockey

What is your favourite thing to do on long bus rides?
Socialize with the guys

Who is your favourite superhero?
Spiderman

What is your favourite NHL team?
The Toronto Maple Leafs and the Detroit Red Wings

Otters in the 4th round, 76th overall, but he made the decision not to play in the OHL.

Living in St. Catharines, Ontario, Riley felt that his best route for a NCAA college scholarship would be to play Junior B in a league that is comparable to most Junior A leagues. For two years, Grade 11 and Grade 12, Sheahan played for the St. Catharines Falcons Junior B team. For two years straight, he led the Falcons in scoring. But it was in his first year with the Falcons that the colleges came knocking on his door. Although he had a few to choose from, he only made one official visit to the University of Notre Dame in Indiana. In the fall of 2009, at just seventeen, Riley started playing college hockey for the Notre Dame Fighting Irish, being one of the youngest players to play college hockey. The Fighting Irish played him in every situation and he had regular shifts, earned a

spot on the power play, and also killed penalties. They were happy with Sheahan and felt that he brought size, speed, and skill to their roster.

Over the year in college hockey, Sheahan turned himself into a strong, two-way player, becoming known as a solid, mature defensive centre with a quick release, a good shot, and great play-making ability. At the end of his first season with the Fighting Irish, his scoring production wasn't huge, but he made up for it by being solid in all three zones. Sheahan is a big guy who is strong on his skates and moves to the net well. He also has good puck protection and reads the play well.

Coming from an extremely athletic family, (his mother Peggy won a Canadian Junior Softball Championship and was an Ontario Women's Basketball All-Star), Sheahan started playing hockey in St.

Here is Sheahan's debut with Hockey Canada at the Men's National Junior Team Summer Development Camp.

CANADA

Catharines, Ontario for the Catholic Youth Organization with the Star of the Sea Red Wings. From the Star of the Sea Red Wings, he quickly moved into playing AAA hockey with the St. Catharines Minor Hockey Association, and then in high school moved into the Junior B league knowing it was the safest bet if he wanted to play college hockey.

Obviously, Sheahan is a young man who doesn't feel he has to follow the path well worn. Over the years some in the hockey world have felt that Sheahan perhaps picked the wrong route and that he hindered his chances at a hockey career by doing so. Proving the naysayers wrong, Riley has stayed calm, level-headed, and focused on his goals. This has allowed him to arrive at the same doorstep as other players his age. He has had his ups and downs, but currently he is on the up as proven by his invite to the Men's National Junior Team Summer Development Camp and his hugely successful Draft day.

Sheahan is known to have a quick release.

Sheahan played for Team Red at the Men's National Junior Team Summer Development Camp in August. He was scoreless in the two games that Red lost.

Sheahan is currently playing college hockey with the University of Notre Dame Fighting Irish.

Season	Event	Team	GP	G	A	Pts	+/-	PIM
		REGULAR SEASON						
2009–10	CCHA	University of Notre Dame	37	6	11	17	–	11
2008–09	Ont. Jr. B	St. Catharines Jr. B Falcons	40	27	46	73	–	55
2007–08	Ont. Jr. B	St. Catharines Jr. B Falcons	45	22	39	61	–	39
TOTALS			122	55	96	151	–	105
		PLAYOFFS						
2009		St. Catharines Jr. B Falcons	11	8	5	13	–	30
2008		St. Catharines Jr. B Falcons	16	5	10	15	–	14
TOTALS			27	13	15	28	–	44

Riley Sheahan

Jeff Skinner

CANADA

Shoots: **Left**

Height: **5'10"**

Weight: **190 lbs**

Birthdate: **May 16, 1992**

Birthplace: **Markham, Ontario**

Hometown: **Markham, Ontario**

Team: **Kitchener Rangers, OHL**

MHA: **Markham Waxers MHA**

2010 NHL Entry Draft:
1st Round, 7th Overall, Carolina Hurricanes

After scoring fifty goals in the 2009–10 season with the Kitchener Rangers, Jeff Skinner finally made the hockey world stand up and take notice. In the fall of 2009, he wasn't really on anyone's radar, and certainly wasn't high on the scouting reports, but fall became winter and his name started to get thrown around.

Jeff Skinner is an elite offensive player and, it's safe to say, that he is a great goal scorer, an offensive talent, and one who scores with style. His fiftieth goal with the Rangers was scored on a breakaway with eleven seconds left on the clock. When the puck hit the back of the net, Skinner became the first Rangers player in twenty-five years to score fifty goals. A keen photographer took a photo of this goal popping in the net and the Rangers cleverly made copies. The copies were sold with the money going to a charity of Skinner's choice. He picked a Hospice in Waterloo.

Added to his fifty goals that season, Skinner also accumulated forty assists for a ninety-point total. The scoring streak continued, and in the 2010 OHL playoffs, Skinner managed to procure twenty goals to lead the league in goals and with thirty-three points to tie for second in overall points. This second place finish was behind number one draft pick, Taylor Hall. Naturally, these point streaks made scouts start talking. In June, at the 2010 NHL Entry Draft, the Carolina Hurricanes didn't hesitate to take Jeff Skinner as their first pick. Although he

Jeff played minor hockey in Markham, Ontario.

Skinner scored fifty goals for the Kitchener Rangers in 2009–10, breaking many records.

What is your favourite movie?
The Dark Knight and 300

What is your favourite
television show?
Friends

What is your favourite book?
The Scarlet Pimpernel

And your favourite magazine?
Sports Illustrated

What is your pre-game meal?
Chicken and pasta

What is your favourite
family meal?
Steak or seafood

What is your favourite subject
in school?
English

What is your favourite band?
I don't have a favourite.
I enjoy listening to all
types of music

What are your favourite activities
outside of hockey?
Hanging out with my
family and dogs, playing
other sports for fun

Who is your hockey hero?
Bobby Orr

Who are your heroes outside
of hockey?
Muhammad Ali and
Terry Fox

What is your most memorable
hockey experience?
Winning the Under-18
Championship and
representing my country

What is your favourite thing
to do on long bus rides?
Watch movies and hang
out with teammates

Who is your favourite superhero?
Batman

What is your favourite NHL team?
The Carolina Hurricanes

is only 5'10", and considered small by some, Skinner went in the 1st round, 7th overall.

Jeff Skinner put on his first pair of hockey skates when he was three years old. At the same time, he also put on figure skates. At the age of five, Skinner was figure skating for the York Region Skating Academy, a competitive club, and he was also playing hockey for the Markham Waxers. What is truly amazing about Jeff is that he was a serious figure skater and an elite hockey player until the age of thirteen. From toe picks to solid blades, he changed his skates to suit the sport without much trouble. Never tripping over his blades, Skinner excelled at both sports. In the same year, (2004), that he placed third to win the bronze medal in the BMO Skate Canada Junior Nationals in juvenile men's he was also named MVP of the Ottawa International peewee AAA tournament. (To put this in perspective, at that same figure skating event, Olympian Patrick Chan won gold in novice men's.) Oh, and Skinner's elite soccer team also won the Ontario Cup that summer. He scored the winning goal.

The decision to give up figure skating and soccer and just play hockey resulted from of an injury. A hit from behind that hurt his knee in a summer league hockey game when Skinner was thirteen forced him to take some time off from figure skating, hockey, and soccer. Suddenly, his family realized just how much he was doing. When September came it was hard for Skinner to return to his

Skinner is a naturally gifted goal-scorer.

Skinner was a competitive figure skater until the age of thirteen.

Skinner at the Men's National Junior Team Summer Development Camp in August.

Jeff Skinner

Jeff could easily switch from figure skates to hockey skates when he was young.

figure skates. But Skate Canada holds nothing against this young man for quitting their sport, and when Skinner went in the 1st round of the 2010 NHL Entry Draft they wrote about him on their website, wishing him the "best of luck at the Carolina Hurricanes conditioning camp this summer."

Although Skate Canada was disappointed with his choice, Hockey Canada couldn't have been more pleased. Skinner has been a solid player for many Hockey Canada teams. In 2009, he played for Team Ontario at the World Under-17 Hockey Challenge, winning a gold medal and scoring the game-winning goal against Russia in the championship final. Skinner then made the jump to Under-18 and was selected to play on the Men's National Under-18 Summer Team and flew overseas to play in the 2009 Ivan Hlinka tournament, where he picked up his second gold medal and scored six goals in four games to lead the team in most goals scored. Most recently, Skinner was invited to attend the Men's National Junior Team Summer Development Camp in August 2010.

Jeff Skinner has risen to the top because of his natural ability to put the puck in the net. If he continues to play his role and develop as an all-around player, he will be a player with a long career in both pro hockey and international hockey.

Enjoying the moment! Skinner went in the 1st round, 7th overall to the Carolina Hurricanes in the 2010 NHL Entry Draft.

Size has never stopped Skinner from being an effective hockey player.

CANADA

SUMMER UPDATE
Skinner played for Team Red at the Men's National Junior Team Summer Development Camp in August. He picked up an assist on the third Red Team goal in the first game.

Season	Event	Team	GP	G	A	Pts	+/-	PIM	
REGULAR SEASON									
2009–10	OHL	Kitchener Rangers	64	50	40	90	7	72	
2008–09	OHL	Kitchener Rangers	63	27	24	51	-5	34	
TOTALS			127	77	64	141	2	106	
PLAYOFFS									
2010	OHL	Kitchener Rangers	20	20	13	33	3	14	
TOTALS			20	20	13	33	3	14	
HOCKEY CANADA									
Season	Event	Team	GP	G	A	PTS	+/-	PIM	
2009	Memorial of Ivan Hlinka	Under 18	4	0	1	1	–	0	Gold
2009	WU17HC	Ontario	6	2	4	6	–	6	Gold

Jeff Skinner

Ryan Spooner

Shoots: **Left**

Height: **5'10"**

Weight: **177 lbs**

Birthdate: **January 30, 1992**

Birthplace: **Ottawa, Ontario**

Hometown: **Kanata, Ontario**

Team: **Peterborough Petes, OHL**

MHA: **Kanata MHA**

2010 NHL Entry Draft:
2nd Round, 45th Overall, Boston Bruins

The headline of an article published on Friday, October 21, 2001 in the *Ottawa Citizen* read, "A Rare Young Talent." The body of the text was about a young nine-year-old named Ryan Spooner who had played thirty-nine games, including exhibition and tournament games, for his team, the Novice B Goulbourn White Rams, and he had already scored upwards of 146 goals. There was even one game when Spooner's team won 20–0 and he scored fifteen of the goals. His parents had been worried that the other players and parents would think it was because they were pushing their son too hard, but that wasn't the reason. In fact, they never pushed him and always let him make his own decisions about hockey. The truth is, in the way that some parents take away video games or television time for discipline Ryan's parents threatened to take away hockey. And Ryan didn't want that, after all, how could he score goals if he couldn't play?

Spooner played minor hockey in Kanata, Stittsville, and Ottawa. When the time came for the 2008 OHL Priority Selection, the Peterborough Petes picked Spooner as their 1st choice, 5th overall. In his first year of play in the OHL as a sixteen-year-old, Ryan came third in Peterborough's scoring and led the Petes rookies in goals, assists, and points. That same year he was eighth in OHL rookie scoring and was named to the OHL Second All-Rookie Team. In his second year with the Petes, Spooner was selected to play on Team Cherry at the 2010

Ryan was known as a rare, young talent when he was young.

Spooner scored the game winning goal for Team Cherry in the 2010 CHL/NHL Home Hardware Top Prospects Game.

Ryan Spooner

Q&A

What is your favourite movie?
The Shawshank Redemption

What is your favourite
television show?
One Tree Hill

What is your favourite book?
To Kill A Mockingbird

And your favourite magazine?
The Hockey News

What is your pre-game meal?
Chicken, rice, and broccoli

What is your favourite
family meal?
Tacos

What is your favourite subject
in school?
History

What is your favourite band?
Modest Mouse

What are your favourite activities
outside of hockey?
Playing table tennis
and Xbox

Who is your hockey hero?
Mario Lemieux

Who is your hero outside
of hockey?
My dad

What is your most memorable
hockey experience?
Playing at the Under-17s
and Under-18s and playing
in the Prospects Game

What's something about yourself
that most people don't know?
I have a dog named Tugger,
after the NHL goalie,
Ron Tugnutt

What is your favourite thing
to do on long bus rides?
Listen to music on my
iPod and sleep

Who are your favourite
superheroes?
Batman and Robin

What is your favourite NHL team?
The Montreal Canadiens
and the Boston Bruins

CHL/NHL Home Hardware Top Prospects Game in Windsor, Ontario, and scored the game-winning goal, helping his team win 4–2. In the spring he took home the William Hanley Trophy as Most Sportsmanlike Player in the OHL for the 2009–10 season.

Many consider Ryan Spooner to be one of those "special players." No, he is not huge, in fact, he comes in at 5'10", but his lack of size doesn't inhibit his play. When he was young he was never the biggest player either, but he had power and skill. There are faster skaters than Spooner, but he has an incredible and rare level of on-ice intelligence that allows him to see things before they happen. This has made him a shifty player, one who has a knack for knowing when to dodge an upcoming check, allowing him to then make the play. It helps that he also has tremendous balance. He is a naturally gifted offensive player and a natural playmaker that finds a way to get the puck to his linemates. For the two years that he has been playing with the Petes, he has worked on his defensive-zone coverage and has improved in this area of play.

Hockey Canada coaches have noticed him and they like how he plays on the big ice surface. In 2009 at the World Under-17 Hockey Challenge, Spooner played for Team Ontario, winning a gold medal and scoring four goals and earning six assists for a total of ten points in six games. Then in August of 2009, he was selected to play in the 2009 Memorial of Ivan Hlinka. He also played at the 2010 IIHF World Under-18 Championship in Belarus, but there was no medal to be had from that tournament as the team finished seventh. Spooner is hoping to have a strong start to the 2010–11 season to garner some interest from the Hockey Canada National Junior Team. Playing for Canada on the World Junior Team would be a dream come true for Spooner, as it is for most young players who work through the Hockey Canada system.

Spooner was selected in the 2nd round, 45th overall by the Boston Bruins at the 2010 NHL Entry Draft because of his strong offensive ability to find the net and score goals. A smaller player like Spooner can have a long hockey career because of his gifted offensive talent, so don't give up on him because of his size. Judging by the way he plays and his success in the sport, he seems to be determined enough to prove any naysayers wrong.

SUMMER UPDATE

Scouts will watch Spooner in the fall as he was not invited to attend the Men's National Junior Team Summer Development Camp.

Spooner has been a solid points-grabber for the Peterborough Petes.

Season	Event	Team	GP	G	A	Pts	+/-	PIM	
REGULAR SEASON									
2009–10	OHL	Peterborough Petes	47	19	35	54	-5	12	
2008–09	OHL	Peterborough Petes	62	30	28	58	-23	8	
TOTALS			109	49	63	112	-28	20	
PLAYOFFS									
2010	OHL	Peterborough Petes	3	0	1	1	-1	2	
2009	OHL	Peterborough Petes	4	0	1	1	-1	0	
TOTALS			7	0	2	2	-2	2	
HOCKEY CANADA									
Season	Event	Team	GP	G	A	PTS	+/-	PIM	
2010	IIHF World Under-18 Championship	Under 18	6	2	0	2	–	2	7th
2009	Memorial of Ivan Hlinka	Under 18	4	1	0	1	–	4	Gold
2009	WU17HC	Ontario	6	4	6	10	–	0	Gold

Tyler Toffoli

Shoots: **Right**

Height: **6'0"**

Weight: **185 lbs**

Birthdate: **April 24, 1992**

Birthplace: **Toronto, Ontario**

Hometown: **Scarborough, Ontario**

Team: **Ottawa 67's, OHL**

MHA: **Toronto Jr. Canadiens MHA**

2010 NHL Entry Draft:
2nd Round, 47th Overall, Los Angeles Kings

The first word out of Tyler Toffoli's mouth when he was learning how to talk was "hockey." Both his father and his uncle were hockey-crazy so this came as no surprise to Tyler's family. At the age of two he had a stick, pads, and used a tennis ball as a puck, and when he was just three he put his boots inside his rollerblades so he could take them on and off himself. And at the age of three he also started playing "real hockey" because his uncle was the coach; he talked the house league into letting his too-young nephew be a member of his team.

So it's safe to say that Tyler loved hockey from a very early age. When Tyler was only twelve, he told his parents that he would be leaving home when he was sixteen to play hockey somewhere on some junior team. Eventually that happened, with the OHL Ottawa 67's.

Toffoli was Ottawa's 1st-round selection, 7th overall in the 2008 OHL Priority Selection draft. Since he had made his decision to go four years prior, Toffoli was ready for the change of scenery and finished his year by leading the Ottawa 67's rookies in goals, assists, and points, was eighth on the team for scoring, sixth in OHL rookie playoff scoring, and was named to the OHL First All-Rookie Team. All in all he had a good first year and adapted well to leaving home. In his second year with the 67's, Toffoli was one of forty CHL players selected to play in the 2010 CHL/NHL Home Hardware Top Prospects game in Windsor, Ontario. He was slotted on Team Orr.

Big smile from Tyler. He played minor hockey with the Toronto Jr. Canadiens.

Toffoli played for Team Orr at the 2010 CHL/NHL Home Hardware Top Prospects Game.

Tyler Toffoli

What is your favourite movie?
Old School

What is your favourite
television show?
Beverly Hills 90210

What is your favourite book?
Twilight

And your favourite magazine?
Sports Illustrated

What is your pre-game meal?
Fettuccine alfredo

What is your favourite
family meal?
Christmas dinner, turkey,
veal, pasta, mashed
potatoes, and veggies

What is your favourite subject
in school?
History

What is your favourite band?
I don't have one, but I like
country music

What are your favourite activities
outside of hockey?
Golf, Xbox, and spending
time with my family

Who is your hero outside
of hockey?
This is an easy one,
my parents

What is your most memorable
hockey experience?
Making the Under-18 Team
Canada and winning gold
at Ivan Hlinka

What's something about yourself
that most people don't know?
I was involved in a charity
commercial for Jake's House
which supports people
with Autism

What is your favourite thing
to do on long bus rides?
Watch movies and sleep

Who is your favourite superhero?
Superman

What is your favourite NHL team?
The Detroit Red Wings and
the Los Angeles Kings

This young, determined player has good hockey sense, reading the play so he can hit the openings. He knows where the puck is going beforehand and is a point-producing player who plays well in big games. Mature beyond his years, Toffoli is extremely independent and comes across as being in charge of his own destiny. Managing his training schedule in the summer months, including working on his skating so he can get to the loose pucks on the ice, will be a key to his success in the future. Now that he has been immersed in the world of major junior hockey, he has seen how much work it takes to progress to the next step, and how important it is to be eat properly and replenish after working out. With his strong mental focus, his desire to win at all costs, and maturity, he will no doubt continue to move up the success ladder.

Toffoli has worn the red and white Hockey Canada jersey more than once. In August of 2009, he donned the jersey when he flew overseas to the Czech Republic to play in the Memorial of Ivan Hlinka Under-18 tournament. Toffoli was a key ingredient to Hockey Canada's gold medal success by scoring three goals and five assists in four games. These stats made him the second-highest scoring leader on the team; he was only edged out by Tyler Seguin. He would have also been selected for the Under-18 team in April but his OHL team, the Ottawa 67's, made it to the second round of the playoffs. Toffoli was also a member of Team Ontario in the 2009 World Under-17 Hockey Challenge, helping his team to win the gold medal by, again, racking up the points. In that tournament, he garnered nine points in just six games. In the spring of 2010, Toffoli managed to snag the big invite from Hockey Canada to attend the Men's National Junior Team Summer Development Camp.

For a young man, Tyler Toffoli has a few championships to his name. He played most of his minor hockey with the Toronto Jr. Canadiens and his team won the Ontario PeeWee Championship, the Ontario Bantam Championship, and the OHL Cup in 2008. Plus, Toffoli was a member of Team GTHL that won the 2007 Tretiak Cup in Russia. In his last year with the GTHL, Toffoli had 174 points in just 83 games.

Tyler Toffoli has many accomplishments to date but look for him to gather even more as he continues to play with the Ottawa 67's and then with the Los Angeles Kings. Toffoli was drafted in the 2010 NHL Entry Draft in the 2nd round, 47th overall, by the Los Angeles Kings. Look out Southern California!

Toffoli has good hockey sense and is known to hit the openings.

Toffoli skating hard for Team Red at the 2010 Men's National Junior Team Summer Development Camp.

SUMMER UPDATE

Toffoli played for Team Red at the Men's National Junior Team Summer Development Camp in August, picking up an unassisted goal in the second game. Red lost both games.

CANADA

Season	Event	Team	GP	G	A	Pts	+/-	PIM	
			REGULAR SEASON						
2009–10	OHL	Ottawa 67's	65	37	42	79	25	54	
2008–09	OHL	Ottawa 67's	54	17	29	46	0	16	
TOTALS			119	54	71	125	25	70	
			PLAYOFFS						
2010	OHL	Ottawa 67's	12	7	6	13	-2	10	
2009	OHL	Ottawa 67's	7	2	6	8	3	4	
TOTALS			19	9	12	21	1	14	

		HOCKEY CANADA							
Season	Event	Team	GP	G	A	PTS	+/-	PIM	
2009	Memorial of Ivan Hlinka	Under 18	4	3	5	8	–	6	Gold
2009	WU17HC	Ontario	6	4	5	9	–	6	Gold

Photo Credits

HOCKEY CANADA IMAGES courtesy of:
Matthew Murnaghan Hockey Canada Images
Andy Devlin HHOF/IIHF Images
Mathew Manor HHOF/IIHF Images
Mika Kylmaniemi HHOF/IIHF Images
Pekka Mononen HHOF/IIHF Images
Jeff Vinnick HHOF/IIHF Images
pg 12, 13, 16, 17, 18, 20, 22, 23, 25, 26, 27, 29, 32, 33, 36, 37, 39, 40, 42, 43, 46, 48, 51, 52, 53, 56, 58, 59, 61, 63, 66, 69, 70, 71, 72, 73, 76, 77, 78, 81, 82, 83, 86, 88, 87, 91, 92, 94, 97, 98, 99, 102, 108, 111, 112, 115, 116, 119, 120, 124, 125, 128, 129, 130, 135, 136, 138, 139, 142, 145 (bottom), 148, 152, 155

OHL IMAGES – Aaron Bell
pg 25, 28, 30, 31, 45, 47, 62, 64, 65, 85, 101, 108, 109, 117, 131, 133, 134,143, 144, 146 (bottom), 147, 149, 151, 153, 154

WHL IMAGES – Courtesy of WHL Photographers
pg 16, 19, 21, 49, 55, 60, 67, 68, 79, 89, 90, 93, 95, 96, 103, 104, 105, 106, 107, 113, 121, 123

QMJHL IMAGES – Karl Jahnke – pg 35,41, 74, 75

QMJHL IMAGE – Steve Déschenes – pg 15

FAMILY PHOTOS:

Domingue Family – pg 12

Teichmann Family – pg 22

Visentin Family – pg 26

Gauthier-Leduc Family – pg 32

Gormley Family – pg 36

Gudbranson Family – pg 42

Petrovic Family – pg 48

Pysyk Family – pg 52, 54, 57

Siemans Family – pg 58

Silas Family – pg 62

Connolly Family – pg 66

Gallagher Family – pg 78

Hall Family – pg 82

Hamilton Family – pg 88

Howden Family – pg 92

Jenner Family – pg 98

Johansen Family – pg 102

Nugent-Hopkins Family – pg 112

Puempel Family – pg 116

Ross Family – pg 120

Schwartz Family – pg 124, 126, 127,

Seguin Family – pg 130,

Sheahan Family – pg 136, 137, 140, 141

Skinner Family – pg 142, 145 (top of page), 146

Spooner Family – pg 148

Toffoli Family – pg 152

FRONT COVER IMAGES (*left to right*)
Hockey Canada Image – Jeff Vinnick HHOF/IIHF Images
WHL Image – Courtesy of WHL Photographers
OHL Image – OHL IMAGES/ Aaron Bell
QMJHL Image – Karl Jahnke